D0354183

American River College Library
4700 College Oak Drive
Sacramento, CA 95841

# contagious success

# contagious success

Spreading High Performance
Throughout Your Organization

SUSAN LUCIA ANNUNZIO
*with* SHARON SUTKER MCGOWAN

PORTFOLIO

PORTFOLIO

Published by the Penguin Group

Penguin Group (USA) Inc., 375 Hudson Street, New York, New York 10014, U.S.A.

Penguin Group (Canada), 10 Alcorn Avenue, Toronto, Ontario, Canada M4V 3B2 ( a division of Pearson Penguin Canada Inc.)

Penguin Books Ltd, 80 Strand, London WC2R 0RL, England

Penguin Ireland, 25 St. Stephen's Green, Dublin 2, Ireland (a division of Penguin Books Ltd)

Penguin Books Australia Ltd, 250 Camberwell Road, Camberwell, Victoria 3124, Australia (a division of Pearson Australia Group Pty Ltd)

Penguin Books India Pvt Ltd, 11 Community Centre, Panchsheel Park, New Delhi–110 017, India

Penguin Group (NZ), Cnr Airborne and Rosedale Roads, Albany, Auckland, New Zealand (a division of Pearson New Zealand Ltd)

Penguin Books (South Africa) (Pty) Ltd, 24 Sturdee Avenue, Rosebank, Johannesburg 2196, South Africa

Penguin Books Ltd, Registered Offices: 80 Strand, London WC2R 0RL, England

First published in 2004 by Portfolio, a member of Penguin Group (USA) Inc.

10   9   8   7   6   5   4   3   2   1

Copyright © Susan Lucia Annunzio, 2004
All rights reserved

PUBLISHER'S NOTE

This publication is designed to provide accurate and authoritative information in regard to the subject matter covered. It is sold with the understanding that the publisher is not engaged in rendering legal, accounting or other professional services, If you require legal advice or other expert assistance, you should seek the services of a competent professional.

LIBRARY OF CONGRESS CATALOGING IN PUBLICATION DATA

Annunzio, Susan Lucia.
    Contagious success : spreading high performance throughout your organization / Susan Lucia Annunzio with Sharon Sutker McGowan.
       p. cm.
    Includes bibliographical references and index.
    ISBN 1-59184-060-0
    1. Organizational effectiveness.  2. Teams in the workplace.  3.  Organizational change.
4. Organizational behavior.  5. Performance.  6.  Success in business.  I.  McGowan, Sharon Sutker.  II. Title.

HD58.9.A545  2004
658.4–dc22      2004053389

This book is printed on acid-free paper. ∞

Printed in the United States of America
Designed by Adam B. Bohannon

Without limiting the rights under copyright reserved above, no part of this publication may be reproduced, stored in or introduced into a retrieval system, or transmitted, in any form or by any means (electronic, mechanical, photocopying, recording or otherwise), without the prior written permission of both the copyright owner and the above publisher of this book.

The scanning, uploading, and distribution of this book via the Internet or via any other means without the permission of the publisher is illegal and punishable by law. Please purchase only authorized electronic editions and do not participate in or encourage electronic piracy of copyrightable materials. Your support of the author's rights is appreciated.

To Sasha, Sharon, George, Richard, John, and Jon—
without whom there would be no book.

*To my children, Christopher and Angie Rose,*
*whose passion and courage*
*embody the next generation of leadership.*

*"When I have been truly searching for my treasure, I've discovered things along the way that I never would have seen had I not had the courage to try things that seemed impossible."*

—Paulo Coelho, *The Alchemist*

This book required doing the impossible. Trusted colleagues told me that it's impossible to study knowledge workers—an ill-defined, hard-to-reach population. They said it's impossible to use the Internet to conduct a study around the world, and it's impossible to prove that valuing people is necessary to make money. But somehow, the high-performing workgroup that I am privileged to lead was able to do the impossible. It was meant to be.

We have an important message to send, a message that affects the lives of many around the globe. The message is that companies must respect and value people. This is a "must have," not a "nice to have."

I write this book honored to be the messenger. I have been a consultant and educator throughout my career. But underneath these titles is a do-gooder wanting to change the world and make it a better place. I believe that the best way to influence the world is through the businesses that make the goods, provide the services, and employ the people who fuel the economy.

My personal mission has been to demonstrate to senior leaders that treating people with respect is a business imperative. I have supported this by sharing my experiences, relating many anecdotes, and quoting other experts. But I didn't have the data to prove my point. Now I do.

How do you spread high performance throughout your organization? The answer is to identify your high-performing workgroups and share their secrets.

Susan Lucia Annunzio
Susan.annunzio@centerforhighperformance.com
November 2004

ACKNOWLEDGMENTS

This is a book about high-performing workgroups. It seems fitting that it was not written by one person, but by a team of extraordinary professionals dedicated to changing the rules of business in the twenty-first century.

Our core group included Richard Day, George Hogenson, Sharon McGowan, John Ross, and Sasha Song. Individually and together, they questioned premises, challenged assumptions, and sought out solutions to the problems we encountered. It is impossible to convey how much this group of people means to me.

My deepest gratitude and affection go to Sasha Song, who has stood by me for nearly a decade. It could be said that I am the "leader" of our team, but it is Sasha who holds the wheel and steers the ship in the right direction. If it were not for Sasha, I would often fail to notice the dangers lurking ahead. Sasha sees the dangers and skillfully guides us around potential disasters.

The people at Richard Day Research in Evanston, Illinois, helped make this book possible through their diligence, relentless perfectionism, and integrity. Special thanks to Richard Day, for his phenomenal leadership, and John Ross, for his sure-footed guidance and patience; and to the rest of the RDR team for their support. They were determined to find a way to do a type of research that had never been done before. Not only did they succeed, they did it extraordinarily well.

Thanks to George Hogenson, who persistently dug deeper into the research findings. He dropped a few bombshells along the way, shattering some of our cherished conclusions and pushing us to get it right.

To Caroline Chubb, Janet Dykstra, Juan Medina, Jackie Spector, and Justin Steele, who assisted the research team with qualitative findings, thank you for persevering. And to Jim Yarnall and Jim McGowan at Desktop Edit Shop, Inc., for their attention to detail and commitment to the project.

My special thanks to our extended team—Jeff Anderson, Graham Alexander, Greg Carlisle, Rick Gray, Larry Hall, Eric Marcus, Andrew McNeilis, Blair Miller, Margaretta Noonan, Mark Smith, Paul Stoltz, and Latham Williams— who helped clarify our message and strengthen our ability to deliver it globally.

I would like to single out Jon Chait, chairman and CEO

of the Hudson Highland Group, Inc., for special appreciation. I have known Jon as a client, a friend, and now as my business partner and "boss." Believing that our small group could make an important contribution in the business community, he had the courage to explore uncharted territory and fund our research. Jon Chait embodies the leadership companies require to drive high performance.

And thanks to the other members of the Hudson Highland senior leadership team—Roberta Andrews, Laurent Chen, Brendan Flood, Bob Goodman, Richard Harris, Anne Hatton, Chris Hermannssen, Michael Kelly, Thomas Moran, Richard Pehlke, and John Wallace—for helping spread the word throughout the world.

More than three thousand individuals participated in our study, and I am deeply grateful to all of them for sharing their time, knowledge, and experience.

I would like to specifically acknowledge a few of the knowledge workers and business leaders who contributed to this book but are not mentioned in the text: Jeff Chris, Bill Deaton, Jennifer Dollapina, Ted Havill, Stephanie Knotts, Jason Louttit, Matt Levin, Cindy Loughridge, Sekayna Mahon, Gus Padres, Matt Payne, Ben Petree, and Roy Wallen.

Additional thanks to Bob Heaton, COO and principal of Macquarie Capital Partners; and Stan Sewitch, managing director of RSM McGladrey, for helping to identify great stories.

To my family—Christopher, the visionary, and Angie

Rose, the dynamo—thank you for your inspiration and for always being there for me. Both rule breakers—distinctively different, distinctively special—they are leaders in their own right. Each will make an important imprint on the world.

Thanks to Larry Hall—again!—this time for being my "big brother." I can always count on you when I need someone to lean on.

I send my love to my parents, knowing both are watching over me. My father, Frank Annunzio, was an outstanding leader in the United States Congress for twenty-eight years. I learned from him how to make change happen. My mother, Angela Alesia, taught me that it is sometimes necessary to accept things the way they are.

Thanks to my friends, in particular Mary Jo Fillipini, Barbara Jean Fitzgerald, Caryle Jerrick, Alexis Sarkisian, and Renee Tracy, for listening to me, believing in me, and helping me to keep believing in myself.

Sincerest thanks to Denise Marcil, my agent and, more importantly, my good friend. Guiding me, prodding me, always looking out for my best interests, she has believed in me for fifteen years despite evidence that might have swayed her convictions. She is a consummate professional—and an extraordinary person.

Thank you to Adrian Zackheim, my publisher, who was willing to back this project even when the research was still incomplete, because he intuitively understood its direction and importance. Adrian's collaboration and critical thinking guided the project from start to finish.

Thanks as well to the team at Portfolio Books, especially Mark Ippoliti and Will Weisser, for doing an outstanding job of bringing this book to market.

My final debt is to Sharon McGowan, my friend and colleague for the past ten years. Coming into the project late, Sharon committed to an impossible timetable and gave up nights, weekends, and time with her family to finish this book on time. She relentlessly asked the questions necessary to close the gaps in my mental leaps. She found a way to make complex research findings and recommendations coherent. Her superb writing skills and rigorous pursuit of the truth made it possible for me to deliver an exceptionally well-executed message. There are no words that can express my appreciation, respect, and affection for Sharon.

The *Contagious Success* Research Team

Back Row (*left to right*): John Ross, George B. Hogenson, Richard Day; front row (*left to right*): Sasha Song, Susan Lucia Annunzio, Sharon S. McGowan. Photo by Greg Carlisle

CONTENTS

# CHAPTER 1

# It's the Workgroup

Success is contagious. That's the premise of this book.

Every company has high-performing workgroups that both make money for the business and develop new products, services, or markets. These workgroups create environments in which results are achieved and people flourish. High-performing groups adapt quickly to changes in the marketplace, understand their customers, and know how to get the internal resources they need to accomplish their goals.

If you spread the secrets of these groups, you can improve the overall performance of your company.

Just as the leaders of Wal-Mart think of their highly successful company as a series of individual stores, you can think of your company, regardless of size, as a series of workgroups. As Robert Slater wrote in *The Wal-Mart Decade*, "... the only way to manage such a large and complex organization is to think of it not as large and complex, but think of it as simply a series of individual units, that is, the stores. 'We run the business a store at a time,' said [David] Glass [president and CEO from 1988 to 2000]. 'How do you run a $240 billion retail business? I don't have a clue. But I know how to run retail stores.' "

How do you run a business in today's uncertain global environment? How do you improve performance in an era of tightening budgets, reduced resources, and increasing demands? The answer is to support your workgroups so they can generate new ideas to fuel profitable growth.

A workgroup can be a few people or a few hundred; it is the unit responsible for driving results. Workgroups can be formed based on functional areas (the marketing department); divisions within functional areas (the creative group); client; or product line. They can be permanent, or temporarily brought together to achieve a single purpose. Workgroups form their own smaller cosmos within the larger company. They are united by common goals and shared experience.

In this book, I will introduce you to some highly successful workgroups. Among others, you will meet:

- the Green Diesel Technology team at International Truck and Engine Corporation, which played a major role in preserving the diesel industry while creating a significant growth opportunity for the company.

- the People and Culture department at Microsoft UK, which helped make the company the United Kingdom's IT employer of choice, and generates 30 percent more revenue per employee than any other division of Microsoft worldwide.
- the Kellogg Food Away From Home marketing department, whose efforts resulted in nearly 10 percent profit growth between 2002 and 2003. Growth due to innovation tripled between 2001 and 2003.
- the Foreign Exchange Institutional Sales team at ABN AMRO, which advises financial institutions on how to optimize returns on currency management. The team was on pace to achieve $20 million in revenue in 2004, up approximately 67 percent from $12 million in 2002.

All of these workgroups have created high-performance environments that deliver exceptional results. Unfortunately, there are too few of such groups. Recent groundbreaking research on the workgroups of knowledge workers found that only 10 percent of these highly paid and well-educated respondents could provide evidence that their workgroup was high performing—that it made money for the company and introduced new products, services, or processes. The study was undertaken by the Hudson Highland Center for High Performance, which I lead. (See Appendix 1 for details on how the research was conducted.)

To increase performance, companies need to focus on the single factor that is most critical to high performance—the environment of their workgroups. According to Daniel Gilbert, professor of psychology at Harvard University, "Four decades of scientific research have shown that situations are powerful determinants of human behavior—and much more powerful determinants than most of us realize."

Gilbert continued, "We are exquisitely social animals who respond instantly to the most subtle demands of our social environments, but because those demands *are* so subtle, we often make the mistake of attributing these responses to internal characteristics such as motives, beliefs, traits, attitudes, desires, and intentions. We tend to think that people 'are the way they act' because we fail to recognize how much of their action is guided, shaped, influenced, and dictated by the situation in which it unfolds."

Instead of concentrating on the environment of their workgroups, too many companies focus on allocating financial capital and deploying human resources. On the financial side, their goal is to achieve the best return on investment, measured by profitable growth, meeting investment community expectations, or increasing shareholder value. Due to limited time and unprecedented pressure, senior leaders expend most of their energy managing the numbers. That often means reducing costs and limiting investments to grow profits.

At the same time, most companies want to be employers of choice, and consequently they don't ignore their people.

By activities such as pay for performance, performance management, leadership development, and training, they reward performance, especially that of high-potential workers. They measure return on human capital based on how successfully they recruit and retain the best and brightest individuals for their workforce.

Managing financial and human capital are necessary activities, but they are not sufficient for high performance. Most companies assume that if they provide their workgroups with reasonable financial targets and the right people, they will automatically be able to achieve a high return on their investment. But this assumption is faulty. To achieve the best return on financial and human capital investment, leaders need to deliberately create workgroup environments that can sustain high performance.

"Changing the situation and shaping the environment—that's what leadership is all about," noted Linda Ginzel, clinical professor of managerial psychology at the University of Chicago Graduate School of Business.

There's no question that individual performance does matter. People need to be trained, developed, and given appropriate rewards and incentives. It is also good business to monitor and measure performance. But individual performance is influenced by the environment. If the best and brightest people are not in the right environment, they will not do their best work. Stars in underperforming workgroups won't shine as brightly.

Michael Jordan was already a star when he joined the

Chicago Bulls. However, it was not until Phil Jackson became head coach that the basketball team started winning championships. Jackson created an environment in which all the members of the team could excel. When Coach Herb Brooks chose college players for the 1980 U.S. Olympic hockey team, he did not select the stars; he chose those who could gel as a team. The United States beat the highly favored Soviet team to win the gold medal, in what *Sports Illustrated* called the "greatest sports moment in the 20th century."

These examples demonstrate that in a team sport, an individual performer cannot win a championship alone. Business is a team sport.

## Times Have Changed

The way workgroups are managed today is critically important—even more so than in the past. This is because times have changed. In the Industrial Age, the assembly line fueled economic success. Business decisions were less complex, competition was clear, and how to make money was more straightforward. Top-down, command-and-control leadership was effective; plant workers needed to follow directions and do precisely what they were told. It wasn't necessary or helpful for them to think creatively to do their jobs.

Today, that model no longer works. The business environment is uncertain, markets are saturated, capital is scarce, industries are consolidated, and products are commoditized. Customers have more choices, so companies have to work harder to understand and meet their needs.

To be sustainable, companies have to grow revenues; cutting costs is not sufficient nor is operational excellence. The only way they can grow revenues is to differentiate themselves by creating new products, services, and markets. Workers can no longer simply follow orders. Now they need to use their brainpower to foster growth.

Whirlpool Corporation, based in Benton Harbor, Michigan, expects all employees to come up with new ways to meet customer needs. "We feel like everyone from the very top of the organization to the people on the manufacturing floors can contribute to driving relationships with our customers," said Donna Samulowitz, Whirlpool's vice president of Global Customer Loyalty.

Samulowitz said that Whirlpool is not abandoning the core strengths that grew the business to where it is today. "Our trade partner relationships and our operational excellence are still critical, but they are not enough. To drive our growth goals, we recognize the importance of customer loyalty, which comes from meeting customers' needs through new products and services, and staying with the customer throughout their relationship with our brands."

Samulowitz added, "It's critical that everybody play a part in driving innovation. Unique solutions can come from anywhere in the organization as long as people have the right focus."

This approach requires leaders to act differently than in the past. The strategies that worked in the Industrial Age are no longer effective. Leaders need to be honest about their own strengths and weaknesses. They must recognize that they can't be or do everything and, therefore, should make sure the people around them have complementary strengths.

"Arrogance is out of fashion in the executive suite. So are autocratic executives who rule by intimidation, think they have all the answers and don't believe they need to be accountable to anyone," wrote Carol Hymowitz in the *Wall Street Journal*. She added that executives who are not willing to share authority and be more accountable "may find themselves passed over for the top job."

Since leaders can't have all the answers, they must rely on others for help. It is most likely that the answers—new services, products, and markets—will emerge from knowledge workers, people who manipulate information and use it to make business decisions.

That's why, when the Hudson Highland Center for High Performance decided to study high performance in companies, we focused on knowledge workers' perceptions of their workgroups. The goal of our research was to identify the "genes" that make up a healthy workgroup. If companies knew what genes distinguish high-performing workgroups from other groups, they would be able to clone those genes to increase overall performance.

Our study of more than three thousand knowledge workers in the United States, Europe (France, Germany, Italy, the Netherlands, Sweden, the United Kingdom), Japan, Australia, Beijing, and Shanghai revealed three factors that are the biggest differentiators between high-performing and nonperforming workgroups. (See Appendix 2 for details about the results in individual regions.) We found a global standard: The genes that enable high performance are consistent around the world.

The major factors that distinguish high-performing workgroups are:

- Valuing people
- Optimizing critical thinking
- Seizing opportunities

*Underlying Premises of the Research*

- To achieve profitable growth, companies need to differentiate through new products, services, and markets.
- Performance is driven by the workgroup, not by the individual.
- Every company, regardless of how profitable or unprofitable, has high-performing workgroups.
- The best individual performers won't do their best work if they are put in the wrong environment.

Not surprisingly, when we asked members of high-performing groups to rate the applicability of a series of statements to their workgroups, they gave the highest scores to the following: "The group learns what customers want;" "our group leader knows our business well;" and "the group meets customer needs." As many experts have argued, companies need to know their business and their customers to succeed. However, that alone won't produce high performance. What differentiates high-performing and nonperforming workgroups is the environment.

The work environment is linked to customer satisfaction. The right work environment results in satisfied employees, and studies have shown a high correlation between employee and customer satisfaction. For example, a frequently quoted University of Michigan study found that the correlation between customer satisfaction and employee satisfaction is .86, with 1.0 being a perfect correlation.

A 1998 *Harvard Business Review* article, "The Employee-Customer-Profit Chain at Sears," discussed a business model that tracks the impact of employee attitudes on customer satisfaction and, ultimately, financial performance. According to the Sears model, improving employee attitudes by five points on the company's survey scale will drive up customer satisfaction by 1.3 points, which in turn leads to a 0.5 percent increase in revenue growth. The authors stated, "These numbers are as rigorous as any others we work with at Sears. Every year, our accounting firm audits them as closely as it audits our financials."

Other companies have found similar correlations. In a 1998 study that tracked employee attitudes and behaviors, customer satisfaction, and profitability, Xerox concluded that employee satisfaction measures are closely linked to customer results. Using data from annual surveys, Northern Telecom of Toronto found "conclusive evidence" that boosting employee satisfaction leads to more satisfied customers and improved financial results.

It is logical to conclude that people who work in environments in which they are valued, can do their best thinking, and have the freedom to seize opportunities are more satisfied with their jobs.

## Value People

The study provides, for the first time, quantifiable proof that there is a direct correlation between how you treat people and financial results. The best way to value people is to create an environment in which smart people are treated as if they are smart. Employees are told what the goals are; they are not told how to achieve them. In these environments, employees have the latitude to make decisions about how to achieve their goals.

At Best Software, a Georgia-based software development company, Bill Furrey's boss put him in charge of developing a new product and then got out of the way. "He let me do my job. He basically said, 'If you need anything, come and talk to me. If you don't, have fun, and go at it.'" Furrey, in turn, trusted his team to accomplish the goal. "I allowed my developers to work and do the job that they needed to do," he said. The team released the product on time, with all the planned features. According to Furrey, management was shocked, because that had never happened before. "It didn't happen on other teams. It did on ours because we really believed in the product and what we were doing."

The ABN AMRO Foreign Exchange Institutional Sales team gives its salespeople the opportunity to interact with various levels of the client organization. "We're given a lot of tools and a lot of information that can enhance our relationship with the client," said Brian Tracy, an associate in the group. "I came into the business knowing little about the foreign exchange market, and I was brought up to speed very quickly."

Robert Rodman, the workgroup leader, explained, "The salesperson is the quarterback of the relationship, pulling resources to address various problems and opportunities. That is unlike other banks that are focusing on institutional clients, where people are very specialized in their roles. In our group, the salesperson has ownership of the overall relationship. . . . They have more authority and autonomy and are privy to a greater understanding of all client issues. That's enabled us to attract higher caliber recruits."

Barrister Executive Suites, Inc., is a California-based private company that leases commercial office space, along with receptionists, furniture, office equipment, and other business needs. The company trusts its property managers to do a good job, and gives them a great deal of authority. "You can run a million dollar business, and you're in charge of the budget; you're in charge of all the hiring and firing at that location, of the equipment, of getting the new tenants," said chairman and CEO Vince Otte. "We have corporate support but basically it is like they have their own business. And that seems to work." The company reduced the number of employees from 135 to 100 and increased annual revenue from $5 million to about $25 million since the current owners took over in 1990.

In high-performing groups, people also have the authority to use resources to meet their goals. "If it's necessary to spend fifty thousand dollars in one night because something is going to blow and a client is not going to be happy, then we spend that fifty thousand dollars because it had to get done and we could have lost a million dollars," one respondent said.

## Optimize Critical Thinking

The second major differentiator between high-performing and nonperforming groups is optimizing critical thinking. Critical thinking involves drawing logical conclusions from complex information and determining how to use that information to achieve the workgroup's goals. To be able to think critically, people need the information to do their best work.

Tom Mendoza, president of Network Appliance, said that his company "made a decision early on that we were going to give our employees too much information. We were going to be too open with them . . . I'm trusting that they will not hurt us with that information." And, in fact, Mendoza said that "we've never been hurt." Network Appliance, a leading network storage solutions company, joined the prestigious *Fortune* list of "100 Best Companies to Work For" in 2003.

Thinking critically also requires people to get their emotions out of the way. If they believe that leaders' words and actions aren't congruent, they react angrily, which distracts them from doing their job and kills motivation.

One study respondent said that in his company there is never enough money for new equipment or upgrades, "but at the same time we're finding out that the CEO got a $12.4 million bonus."

In another company, executives are asking employees to cut costs by turning off lights, flying coach, and staying in inexpensive hotels. In the meantime, the executives enjoy weekly catered lunches, fly first class to meetings at the drop of a hat, and take limousines two miles to the airport. The company used to stock ramen noodles for people who work late at night but stopped doing that, presumably to save money. "Ramen only costs ten cents. And it's good for six to seven months. So, you have all these developers who no longer work late at night because there's no food in the kitchen," said a study participant.

## Seize Opportunities

The third gene identified in high-performing workgroups is the ability to seize opportunities. This requires a learning environment in which people can take risks, generate new ideas, and make mistakes. That, in turn, leads to new products, services, and markets.

The marketing group at UNITE, a U.K.–based owner and manager of student housing, saw an opportunity to generate new revenue after conducting customer research that identified the need for high-speed broadband Internet access for residents. The group jumped on the idea and entered into a partnership with a telecom supplier to provide the new service. The company expects to generate more than £2 million in sales revenue in the first year of the agreement. "It's considered to be a great business opportunity," noted Rachel Bateson, marketing manager at UNITE.

GreenHouse Communications, a fifteen-year-old marketing communication firm, encourages continual learning. "The reason our company is still going when many agencies like ours have folded is pathological tenacity. Whether it's overcoming marketplace challenges or challenges our clients face, we don't give up until we've found a way to make it work," said Sandy House, chairman and CEO.

A learning environment can foster unexpected positive results. For example, Pfizer reaped $1.7 billion in sales from Viagra in 2002, which got its start as a potential treatment for a heart condition. As *BusinessWeek* reported in a 1998 cover story, "The New Era of Lifestyle Drugs," "Ironically, the drug now at the forefront of all this ferment was discovered more by serendipity than fancy chemistry. Pfizer researchers were investigating the compound, technically known as sildenafil citrate, for angina in men when they heard that study participants reported an unexpected side effect: the drug was improving their sex lives." Instead of concluding that their work on angina was a failure, they seized a new opportunity.

Bright Horizons Family Solutions, Inc., a workplace child-care center business headquartered in Watertown, Massachusetts, turned a serious challenge into an opportunity during the 1990s. "Unemployment dropped and we had a terrible problem hiring enough teachers. Child care was so undervalued, people could make more money in any other profession," explained company cofounder and chairman Linda Mason.

As a result, many child-care businesses were forced to fold. However, Bright Horizons used the shortage of workers as an opportunity to become more sophisticated and creative in its recruiting strategies. Up until that time, the company primarily recruited early childhood majors on college campuses. "We began to actively target seniors and empty nesters," said Mason. "We also targeted immigrants. . . . There are lots of immigrants who are highly educated, but have limited job options. That's when we developed our own internal training and accreditation program. Our recruiting function has become more sophisticated, broad, and creative," Mason said.

Valuing people, optimizing critical thinking, and seizing opportunities enable high performance. Our study also found that the single biggest impediment to high performance around the world is short-term thinking. To meet quarterly financial goals, companies are trying to do more with less, overworking their people, and cutting muscle along with the fat. Regrettably, they may be sacrificing long-term sustainability for short-term results.

The study identified groups that were once high performing but no longer are. These groups may have once gotten strong financial results by understanding the business and meeting customer needs, but they were unable to sustain these results because they didn't create the right environment. On the other hand, there are workgroups that create the right environment but haven't made the numbers. The key to sustainability is to get results the right way. The more workgroups that get results the right way, the better your company's performance.

In the chapters ahead, I will detail the findings of the largest-ever global study of knowledge workers. You'll learn how to build a work environment that drives high performance, what you can do to improve the performance of your best workgroups, how to "move the middle," and what turns high-performing workgroups into "used-to-be's."

In today's world of increasing demands and unprecedented pressure, business leaders naturally go back to their comfort zone—doing what they have always done, but doing it harder and faster. I think there is a different way. As Jim Collins wrote in his best-selling book, *Good to Great*, "I offer everything herein for your thoughtful consideration, not blind acceptance. You're the judge and jury." As part of your deliberations, I ask you to think about whether you would lead and manage differently if you had proof that the following statements were true:

- There is a quantifiable correlation between profitable growth and the respectful treatment of employees.
- Focusing on productivity alone decreases performance.
- Hard work and high expectations only pay off when people feel valued.
- Strategic planning produces the highest financial return when people are encouraged to take risks.
- Creating a process for high-performing workgroups to share their secrets can increase the number of such groups.

The remainder of this book provides the proof. The rest is up to you.

## Key Points

- Every company has high-performing workgroups that make money for the business and develop new products, services, or markets. If you spread the secrets of these groups, you can improve the overall performance of your company.
- To increase performance, companies need to focus on the single factor that is most critical to high performance—the environment of their workgroups.
- To succeed, companies need to know their business and their customers well—but that alone won't produce high performance.

## Unexpected Findings

- Only 10 percent of global knowledge workers, the highest paid and best educated workers in the world, could provide evidence that their workgroup was high performing.
- We found a global standard—three characteristics that consistently distinguish high-performing workgroups around the world. They are: valuing people, optimizing critical thinking, and seizing opportunities.
- The single biggest impediment to high performance is short-term focus.

# CHAPTER 2

# Look Within

Your company already has right-sized, cut costs, improved efficiency, acquired or shed businesses, and flattened the organization. Yet the path to sustaining profitable growth remains elusive.

Fortunately, however, you don't need to look far for the key to sustainable growth. Within your organization, certain workgroups consistently demonstrate high performance. These are the groups that come up with new products, services, markets, or processes. They contribute to financial results. They seize opportunities. They overcome unexpected challenges and perform well in good economic times or bad.

As I discussed in Chapter 1, workgroups are the fundamental building blocks of success in a company. They can be large or small, a single department or cross-functional team. They can be permanent or ad hoc.

If you knew what factors distinguish your high-performing workgroups from other groups, you could use that information to increase the performance of your entire organization. Your best groups could get even better—you could replicate their best practices, spreading their secrets to under-performing groups in your organization. You also could avoid inadvertently doing things that destroy the work environment and negatively affect the bottom line.

All companies, no matter how well or badly they perform overall, have high-performing groups. For example:

**The Green Diesel Technology Team** at International Truck and Engine Corporation has accumulated an impressive list of accomplishments in the last five years that saved the company from potential disaster. The Illinois-based company, a subsidiary of Navistar International Corp., manufactures commercial trucks, school buses, and mid-range diesel engines.

The cross-functional Green Diesel team started to meet after a potentially precedent-setting ruling by California's air pollution board that diesel fuel was a toxic air contaminant. The board effectively banned light-duty diesel vehicles such as small pickup trucks and SUVs from being sold in the state because they did not meet emission standards. The team members recognized that a total ban on diesel fuel was not out of the question.

To protect the future of diesel, the fuel would have to become as environmentally acceptable as gasoline, they reasoned. Rather than fight the pollution control agencies, they decided to advocate for a solution that would reduce particulate emissions from diesel fuel. Low-sulfur diesel fuel—combined with particulate traps—makes it technologically feasible for diesel to achieve low emission levels that are otherwise not possible.

The Green Diesel team took the lead in convincing the Environmental Protection Agency that for diesel air emissions to go way down, it would have to mandate low-sulfur fuel. In 2001, the EPA ruled that the sulfur content of diesel fuel in trucks and buses must be reduced 97 percent by 2007. To meet emission standards, trucks also will need to have diesel particulate traps.

The solution advocated by the Green Diesel team not only significantly improves the environment, but favors the marketing of the company's particulate filter retrofit kits. In their first year on the market, sales of the kits totaled $7 million, and that's just the beginning. Demand for the retrofit kits is expected to increase when low-sulfur fuel is available everywhere. The kits are the single biggest growth area in the company.

The Green Diesel team introduced the first low-emitting diesel product in the country—the Green Diesel Technology school bus—and scientifically demonstrated that school buses using this technology have lower emissions than buses powered with compressed natural gas. Diesel is now part of the environmental solution and talk of banning it has virtually disappeared.

People who work on the Green Diesel Technology team

are still responsible for their "day jobs," and receive no extra compensation for their efforts. So why do they do it? According to Michele Smith, general counsel of the Engine Group, "The reward is the result."

**The People and Culture** department at Microsoft UK took a company that was perceived as an unattractive employer and transformed it into one of the most sought-after workplaces in the United Kingdom. Microsoft UK made the *Sunday Times* (London) list of "Best Companies to Work For" in 2004.

When Stephen Harvey, who had been director of Finance, took over as director of People and Culture, he focused on making sure that everything the company did on the people side had a business reason. "If it's not there to support the business and what we're trying to achieve at a company level, then we don't do it. It's not soft and fluffy HR anymore; it's got real business value," Harvey said.

The People and Culture team members began to take a new approach to their work. "HR people have a tendency to say 'all we do is hire people; we're not really a profit center,'" Harvey said. "But for the company to achieve its long-term vision, we have to get the people here." The team began to make the connection between effectively managing human capital and successfully executing Microsoft's overall strategy.

The team devised a plan to make Microsoft UK the employer of choice in the IT business, which included creating an environment where great people have a chance to do their best work every day. "That picture of perfection is what drives my HR team," Harvey said.

By knowing who the company's star performers are and focusing on them—making sure they are paid well, challenged, and work with good managers—the People and Culture department makes a major impact on the company. As a result, Microsoft UK is bringing in 30 percent more revenue per employee than any other division of Microsoft worldwide.

**The Midlands Development** team at UNITE Group PLC increased profits tenfold between 2001 and 2003, from about £2 million to £20 million. During the same period, the team added people and expanded its geographical reach. It is an example of a group that worked hard to become a cohesive unit and help the company move closer to its goal of profitability by the end of 2004.

UNITE, based in the United Kingdom, develops, owns, and manages affordable residences for students and government health-care workers. It has grown quickly since its inception in 1991. The Midlands team is one of several regional teams responsible for planning new projects, finding sites, and overseeing construction.

One factor that distinguishes UNITE from its competitors is that it constructs buildings from prefabricated modules. The modules are less expensive to produce and assemble than standard building materials.

The Midlands team was first to roll out the modular system. The team put together a standardized design and construction plan that laid out the steps from the factory to the finished product. It then ran training sessions for its contractor partners, who had never worked with this type of modular product before. If experience at the construction site necessitated a change in the product design, that information was relayed to the factory.

At the same time, the development team worked with other UNITE divisions, including Accommodation Services, a division responsible for property management. "They are essentially the pump that drives cash back into our business," said Tim Mitchell, former regional development director for the Midlands team. Mitchell now directs the Southwest development team.

The people in Accommodation Services and in Regional Development are go-getters, aggressive, and sometimes even pushy. Managing interactions between the two groups can be tricky, Mitchell said. But making the relationship work was important to the Midland team's success, as well as the success of the company.

So instead of negotiating in a take-it-or-leave-it fashion, the Midlands team members set out to take a nonconfrontational approach to interactions and build personal relationships. As a result, Mitchell said, when a difficult issue arose, the Accommodation Services people weren't saying to themselves, "Oh, no, here comes Tim . . . he wants me to agree to something or sign something." Instead the two groups built a positive relationship, which helped get things done.

The Midlands team was able to cultivate successful relationships with other groups because it had already figured out how to enable its own disparate group of individuals to come together as a team.

Mitchell explained, "The team started out as a group of people who'd previously been working in different functions." At his prompting, team members decided to get away from the office and develop strategies for conducting business, such as instituting regular weekly team meetings and sending out advance agendas for project meetings. Realizing that all the company's regions were facing the same issues, the team developed a two-page due diligence checklist for conducting development deals.

In addition, the team threw away its old hierarchical model and reorganized itself horizontally. According to Mitchell, "I said 'let's pretend we're all part of an independent development company and we're all board directors of this development company. . . . There's nobody here that is a junior employee or a senior employee.' "

**The Client Implementation team** at Cendian is a high-performing workgroup in a company that is not yet profitable. A wholly owned subsidiary of Eastman Chemical, Cendian became a $1 billion company less than five years after its inception in 2000. Although the company has had a meteoric rise in revenue growth, profitability has been inconsistent. However, the Client Implementation group has been consistently high performing. The group plays a critical role in the company's business of providing logistics solutions to chemical and plastics customers. The team works with clients from the moment of sale to the time that Cendian takes over their logistics function.

While the sale is clearly important, until the high-performing unit carries out the implementation, Cendian doesn't see the revenue.

For the implementation to go smoothly, the group needs to work with other parts of the company to resolve multiple technical and financial issues quickly and efficiently. "We make sure that we engage the right parties within Cendian to come up with the best solution for the client; we also may engage our suppliers, who are strategic business partners, and we'll engage the client in developing the solution," said Sheryl Chin, senior manager of the group.

A great deal of work goes into understanding what is unique about each client. Team members spend three entire days on site learning about the client's business, so they can plan the right solution instead of trying to fix things after the fact.

Typically, implementation takes six months. However, one recent implementation project was accomplished in a record five weeks. "It delivered early savings of about a million and a half dollars for the client and had significant implications for Cendian as well," said Chin. The quicker the implementation, the faster customers begin realizing cost savings and the faster Cendian accrues revenue. The project represented $40 million in revenue for the company.

Another large-scale implementation of between $80 million to $100 million in volume was accomplished in two months. The customer is expected to save about $600,000 on the initial implementation.

The Client Implementation group has a large responsibility because of the nature of Cendian's business. "When the handoff [of the logistics from the customer to Cendian] doesn't happen just right, all kinds of ugly things could happen because we're shipping bulk chemicals all over the world. Even our smallest clients have operations that are outside the United States so they're pretty complex businesses and sending the wrong stuff to the wrong place is not only just bad, it could be dangerous," said Mark Kaiser, who was CEO at the time of my interview.

Members of the Client Implementation workgroup relish the challenge and are very proud of what they do. "I've been engaged in implementations that span the world and I can't put it into words how it probably would have taken someone ten years to be engaged with that many countries and implementation projects in their career, and I was able to do that in eight months," said Chin.

**The Professional Services group** at VA Software also is a high-performing workgroup in a company that is not yet profitable. VA Software, a Fremont, California–based public company that provides a global software development platform to Fortune 1000 companies, has generated new revenue and profits by developing innovative services. The team is responsible for providing training, deployment, installation, and consulting to the company's customers. More than 800,000 developers use VA Software's open source community Web site, SourceForge.net.

The Professional Services group helped increase SourceForge license and services revenue by 71 percent from January 2003 to January 2004. This has contributed to reducing the company's quarterly loss from 7 cents per share to 2 cents per share during the same time period.

The group also has generated revenue by quickly meeting customer needs. When an important customer asked for additional features and functionality for a recent software release, the Professional Services group pulled together a cross-functional team of customer support and product development professionals to respond.

The team fulfilled the request within a few weeks and communicated effectively with the customer, which led to a license order of more than $300,000 during the same quarter. In addition, the customer began negotiating with VA Software for an enterprise-wide license agreement.

## Landmark Study

While they operate in different industries and serve different functions, all of the groups described above have achieved excellent results in difficult times. They have made money for the company and done something new. Over the years, I have seen many high-performing workgroups in action. I have always been intrigued about what sets them apart.

What is it about their environment that leads to consistently excellent results? Do they have anything in common? Are there certain factors that clearly differentiate them from nonperforming groups? Are they achieving peak performance? Can their secrets be replicated? Although I had theories about the answers to these questions, they were based on anecdotal evidence, not on rigorous research.

To address these questions and quantify what drives high performance in their workgroups, the Hudson Highland Center for High Performance conducted the largest and most in-depth global study ever of knowledge workers. (See Highlights of High-Performance Study, page 31.) More than 5.5 million subscribers to Internet panels around the world were screened to identify more than three thousand qualified participants.

In conjunction with its parent company, Hudson Highland Group Inc., and Richard Day Research, the Center set out to learn what factors accelerate or stifle high performance. In studying how knowledge workers perceive their workgroups, our goal was to better understand what companies could do to compete successfully in the future.

In these uncertain times of increased competition and ubiquitous information, companies must differentiate themselves through new products, services, or markets to grow profitably. While good ideas can come from anywhere, it is most likely that these innovations will emerge from knowledge workers, people who manipulate information and use that information to make business decisions. Knowledge workers drive most of the business results in a company.

In knowledge-intensive industries, such as professional services, pharmaceuticals, and financial services, the cost of labor can be the single greatest operating expense, typically as much as 80 percent. Consequently, high return on this investment is imperative.

But our Internet-based survey of knowledge workers in the United States, Europe (France, Germany, Italy, the

*Highlights of High-Performance Study*

- Largest ever systematic, global study of knowledge workers
- Screened Internet panels of 5.5 million subscribers
- Identified more than 3,000 qualified participants globally
- Participants represented highest paid, best educated, and most highly recruited employees
- Income was in top 10 percent of participants' respective countries
- Thirty percent of the companies in the global Fortune 500 participated

Netherlands, Sweden, the United Kingdom), Japan, Australia, Beijing, and Shanghai found that organizations are not getting the performance from these workers that one would expect by virtue of their education, experience, and salaries.

For example, the study found that knowledge workers are primarily using their intellectual capital to increase efficiencies, rather than focus on innovations such as new products and services. Forty percent of knowledge workers could point to a process improvement for which their workgroup was responsible, compared to only 17 percent who said their group had developed a new product or service. Of course companies need to reduce costs, and process improvements help do that. But reducing costs is not enough. To increase shareholder value, your company is going to have to grow. If only 17 percent of your knowledge workers are developing something new, that's not going to happen.

The research confirmed what I've seen in my MBA and executive education classes at the University of Chicago Graduate School of Business, and at INSEAD, a top-tier business school in Fontainebleau, France. When I ask groups of twenty-five to forty business people whether their company maximizes their brainpower, often no more than two or three raise their hands. This is particularly disappointing in executive education classes, since students typically are top performers hand-picked by their companies.

Participants in the Hudson Highland Center for High Performance study represented the highest paid, most highly recruited, and best educated employees in the world. They came from a wide range of industries. They were employed full time in managerial, professional, or technical occupations, and, at minimum, had the equivalent of a U.S. bachelor's degree. Their income was in the top 10 percent of their respective country or region.

At least 30 percent of the companies in the global Fortune 500, including Foster's Group, Goldman Sachs, Intel, Microsoft, Nippon Steel, Pfizer, and Sony, participated in the research. People in the study represented fifty of the largest one hundred companies in their respective countries or regions, with the possible exception of Europe. (In Europe, we were prohibited by law from asking survey participants where they worked, but it's reasonable to assume that the profile of companies is the same as in the United States, Asia, and Australia.)

One of the study's major findings is that knowledge workers' perceptions of their own workgroups do not match reality. Asked whether their workgroup is high performing (Does it adapt to changing conditions and consistently exceed performance goals and peer group performance?), 77 percent of respondents said yes.

However, when asked to provide evidence of the workgroup's high performance (Did it make money for the company and introduce new products, services, or processes?), only 10 percent could do so. This startling finding

means that 90 percent of the highest paid and best educated employees in the world are not in high-performing
workgroups. Remember, respondents were not a random
group of workers. They are the people most critical to the
success of an organization.

The global distribution of workgroups was 10 percent
high performing, 52 percent average performing, and 38
percent nonperforming. (See Global Distribution of Workgroups, below.) Average-performing groups were able to
provide evidence of performance in at least one of nine areas (profit, revenue, process improvement, product improvement, customer satisfaction, teamwork, safety, social
responsibility, or "other"). Those in nonperforming workgroups could not provide evidence of performance in any of
those areas.

The global distribution of workgroups is consistent with
my own observations of companies across industries and
countries. It suggests that a similar distribution exists at
the company level.

Nonperforming workgroups have not necessarily been

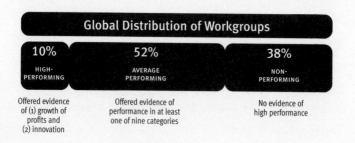

**Global Distribution of Workgroups**

| 10% | 52% | 38% |
|---|---|---|
| HIGH-PERFORMING | AVERAGE PERFORMING | NON-PERFORMING |
| Offered evidence of (1) growth of profits and (2) innovation | Offered evidence of performance in at least one of nine categories | No evidence of high performance |

that way forever. Of the respondents in nonperforming workgroups, 29 percent said that their group performed at a higher level in the past than it does today. This clearly has a negative impact on morale. Imagine the positive financial implications if those workgroups were operating at peak levels! Something happened in those groups that got in the way of their performance. In each of the countries or regions except Japan, the single biggest reason for the drop in performance was poor management or leadership. These groups are too dependent on a single leader, a problem I will discuss in Chapter 4, "Room to Grow."

## Productivity Versus Performance

Seventy-seven percent of respondents in our study said their workgroup is high performing, but only 10 percent are actually in high-performing workgroups. This suggests respondents are confusing performance with productivity. They are working harder than ever; but unfortunately that does not mean they are high performing. "Doing more with less" doesn't mean getting better results.

There was a time when productivity equaled performance. In an industrial economy, it is relatively straightforward to measure productivity by comparing output—for example, the number of cars coming off an assembly line— against the number of hours worked to produce those cars. Today, when the services sector employs 80 percent of the private work force, productivity is much more difficult to measure.

Stephen S. Roach, chief economist for Morgan Stanley, has pointed out that government statisticians use worker compensation to approximate output in many service industries, "which makes little or no intuitive sense."

Units of work time also are out of touch with reality in the professional and managerial segments. "Courtesy of a profusion of portable information appliances (laptops, cell phones, personal digital assistants, etc.) along with near ubiquitous connectivity (hardwired and now increasingly wireless), most information workers can toil around the clock. The official data don't come close to capturing this cultural shift," Roach wrote in *The New York Times*.

By underestimating the time actually spent on the job, we overestimate white-collar productivity. "Productivity is not about working longer. It's about getting more value from each unit of work time. . . . Productivity growth is sustainable when driven by creativity, risk-taking, innovation and, yes, new technology. It is fleeting when it is driven by downsizing and longer hours," Roach wrote. My own experience shows that managers who solely emphasize productivity tend to drive out the capacity in their workers to engage in innovation and creativity. If we encourage productivity and inadvertently drive out innovation, what have we gained?

Our study strongly suggests that leaders in the twenty-first century will have to optimize performance, not just seek to optimize productivity. Knowledge workers, by definition, cannot provide full value to their organization simply through productivity increases. They must constantly seek to extend the horizons of their work and understanding.

To increase shareholder value and sustain profitability, companies must continually encourage their knowledge workers to combine traditional productivity with innovation. In other words, they should foster the creativity that, combined with productivity, leads to high performance. Because complex decisions require the thinking of many people, companies have to focus on managing the workgroup to optimize performance. It is highly unlikely that single individuals will be able to develop the innovations required in the future.

Workgroups respond to a variety of factors that are not typically associated with managing individuals. While compensation, benefits, and similar individual rewards are important, high performance is far more dependent on the environment in which the group is functioning. For example, when we asked knowledge workers in high-performing groups how their group became high performing, pay/compensation was consistently ranked fifth, behind factors such as values, teamwork, people, and planning.

Respondents in high-performing groups ranked rewarding for performance low in the study; however, nonfinancial recognition rated higher than financial recognition. Paying for workgroup performance was a slightly bigger differentiator between high-performing and nonperforming groups than paying for individual performance. Consequently, if you want a quick hit to improve performance, start by increasing nonfinancial recognition and financial recognition for group performance.

Environmental factors tend to be viewed as intangible or soft, yet the study revealed that the environment is central for managing workers in the knowledge economy. As Stephen Harvey, director of People and Culture at Microsoft UK, explained, "You've got to get the people side of the business right to have any chance of getting the customer and partner experience right. Without the customer and partner experience being in great shape, you're not going to get long-term profitability and growth, and increase shareholder value or stakeholder value."

The good news is that 10 percent of workgroups are getting it right. To improve overall performance, it is essential for companies to understand what differentiates these groups—what factors are critical for them to be able to make money and do new things for the business. By understanding what makes high-performing workgroups different, you can improve the results of those groups that already are high performing, prevent them from becoming "used-to-be's," and multiply high performance throughout the company.

Our study uncovered a consistent standard for a high-performance environment in workgroups throughout the world. In Chapter 3, I'll examine the three factors that distinguish these environments and show you how these factors play out in highly successful workgroups.

For the first time ever, we have been able to quantify the

correlation—around the world—between the respectful treatment of workers and the company's ability to increase revenues and profits. We have proved what we suspected from observing companies such as Starbucks and Southwest Airlines: Treating people well makes money.

## Key Points

- Within your organization, certain workgroups consistently demonstrate high performance. These are the groups that come up with new products, services, markets, or processes. All companies, no matter how well or badly they perform overall, have high-performing groups.

- The Hudson Highland Center for High Performance conducted the largest and most in-depth global study ever of knowledge workers. Participants in the study represented the highest paid, most highly recruited, and best educated employees in the world. At least 30 percent of the companies in the global Fortune 500, including Foster's Group, Goldman Sachs, Intel, Microsoft, Nippon Steel, Pfizer, and Sony, participated in the research.

- While good ideas can come from anywhere, it is most likely that innovations will emerge from knowledge workers.

  —In many industries, knowledge workers drive 80 percent of the business results in a company.

  —In knowledge-intensive industries such as professional services, pharmaceuticals, and financial services, the cost of labor is extraordinarily high, and the need for high return on investment is great.

- To increase shareholder value, companies must continually encourage their knowledge workers to combine traditional productivity with innovation.

## Unexpected Findings

- One of the study's major findings is that respondents' perceptions do not match reality. Asked whether their workgroup is high performing (Does it adapt to changing conditions and consistently exceed performance goals and peer group performance?), 77 percent of respondents said yes. When asked to provide evidence of the workgroup's high performance (Did it make money for the company or do anything new?), only 10 percent could do so.

- Nonperforming workgroups have not necessarily been that way forever. Of those respondents in nonperforming workgroups, 29 percent said that their group used to perform at a higher level than it does today.

- The study found that knowledge workers are primarily using their intellectual capital to increase efficiencies, rather than focus on creating new products and services. Forty percent of knowledge workers could point to a process improvement that their workgroup was responsible for, compared to only 17 percent who said their group had developed a new product or service.

- While compensation, benefits, and similar individual rewards are important, high performance is far more dependent on the environment in which the group is functioning.

- Respondents in high-performing groups ranked rewarding for performance low in the study; however, nonfinancial recognition rated higher than financial recognition. Paying for workgroup performance was a slightly stronger differentiator between high-performing and nonperforming groups than paying for individual performance.

CHAPTER 3

# Build It and They Will Come

Every company wants to be an employer of choice. The most exciting finding of our research is that the factors that make people want to work for you are also the biggest differentiators between high-performing and nonperforming workgroups. To sustain profitable growth, you need to create an environment where people feel valued, can do their best thinking, and have the latitude to seize opportunities as they arise. This environment allows high performance to spread throughout your organization, and makes the best and brightest want to come and stay.

The Hudson Highland Center for High Performance identified this environment by asking global survey participants to rate a series of statements about their workgroups. We then compared the ratings of those in high-performing groups with those in nonperforming groups, and identified the biggest differentiators. To better understand what drives high performance we used a statistical technique called factor analysis, which helped identify patterns of behavior in successful workgroups. (For details on this process, see Appendix 3.)

People want to work where they can do their best thinking and are valued for seeking and trying new ideas. Like Sheryl Chin, they want to be part of something that matters to the company and matters to them. "Each day when I come to work I am making an impact on Cendian's bottom line and I am contributing to the service of our clients," said Chin, senior manager, Client Implementation, for Cendian, an Atlanta-based chemical logistics company. "There's absolutely nowhere else that I could have worked and gained this level of experience in such a short period of time. I've been involved in implementations that have resulted in millions of dollars in revenue for the company," Chin added.

*The High-Performance Environment:*
*Necessary but Not Sufficient*

· Hard work and high expectations
· Reward for performance
· Having a plan and measuring against goals

## High-Performing Workgroups

Like Cendian's Client Implementation team, the Kellogg Food Away From Home marketing department is a good example of a workgroup where people feel valued and seize opportunities as they arise. The group has created an environment in which knowledge workers are encouraged to use their brainpower to earn money for the company.

When the marketing group took the Great Place to Work survey recently, it scored 91 out of 100 on the statement "Taking everything into account, I would say this is a great place to work." On five specific measures—credibility, respect, fairness, pride, and camaraderie—the group scored an average of 81.6.

The Kellogg Food Away From Home division, based in Illinois, has shown consistent growth over the past several years. Between 2002 and 2003, revenue grew 3.2 percent and profits grew 9.8 percent. The division markets to convenience stores, drug stores, and fast-food establishments such as McDonald's.

Tammy Gianfortune, vice president of marketing for Kellogg Food Away From Home, deliberately seeks the opinions of group members when making important decisions. For example, in trying to determine a customer bid price recently, Gianfortune consulted one person on the team "who always takes the customer view," in addition to finance and salespeople. "I try to capitalize on people's strengths. I try to get a balanced view," she said. She values people both for their functional expertise and their natural strengths, such as the ability to see things from another person's perspective.

Gianfortune acknowledges that one of the company's values—"assume positive intent"—is not her strength, so she relies on others in her group to point out the positive intent of people's actions. Gianfortune also encourages a learning environment in which her team takes risks after analyzing the ramifications and developing contingency plans.

Recently, for example, the group decided not to continue to pursue a piece of high-volume business that was not profitable. The decision resulted in a top-line loss, but increased profits. The move was clearly risky. "We didn't know it would play out that way. We could have lost a ton more volume than we had projected," Gianfortune said.

Had that happened, the group would have found a way to benefit from the experience. "If it doesn't work, let's figure out what we did right, figure out what we did wrong, and learn from it. . . . We won't make that mistake again," Gianfortune said. The important thing is not to stifle the kind of thinking that went into the plan, she added.

In 2001, about 1.3 percent of the division's sales were attributable to innovations in product development and strategic alliances; in 2003 that figure more than tripled to about 5 percent. One of the most successful new products,

Cereal in a Cup, was introduced in 2001 after the marketing group saw an opportunity to repackage an existing product and make money for the company. The Food Away From Home division sold approximately $36 million (consumer retail value) of the portable breakfast for adults in 2003.

Other recent innovations were strategic alliances with a melba toast and a crouton manufacturer. By forging the alliances, the marketing group filled voids in its product portfolio and was able to better serve its customers. Growth in the core business has accompanied the successful innovations. The division boasts number-one market share in eleven of its fifteen categories and has consistently gained share in recent years.

The Foreign Exchange Institutional Sales team at ABN AMRO is a start-up workgroup at one of the world's largest and well-established banks. The team advises financial clients such as hedge funds, asset managers, commodity trading advisors, and pension funds on how to optimize returns on currency management. The team was on pace to achieve revenues of $20 million in 2004, up approximately 67 percent from $12 million in 2002. The group also ranked third in market share with North American institutional clients, according to *FX Week*'s 2003 Annual Survey.

The new line of business was started in 2002, growing out of the bank's expertise with corporate clients. The high-performing group has implemented several innovations that add value to clients, according to Robert Rodman, managing director and global head of foreign exchange sales to financial institutions and the public sector. Among these is a strong customer focus across the whole spectrum of services, which includes research, strategy recommendations, analytical firepower, and trade execution.

"We have aligned our research strategy to be consistent with the way our clients view the world," Rodman said. "Rather than giving clients a blanket forecast, we provide a forecast relevant to the way they manage their portfolio." In other words, the bank's knowledge workers collect and decipher information to help clients make the best business decisions.

"We have spent countless hours in front of clients to help them improve investment performance, improve the investment process, and grow their firms. We understand how they view the world, and screen information the way they would," Rodman said.

Rodman also created a new group, Foreign Exchange Analytics, that is made up of quantitatively oriented individuals with industry experience in managing foreign exchange risk. "This is a SWAT team that focuses the firm's resources on specific client issues or problems. If we can give them empirically supported trade ideas and provide thought leadership and number-crunching muscle to help them resolve 'what if' scenarios and resolve problems, we are two-thirds of the way to being meaningful," Rodman said.

The last piece of the puzzle is to partner with clients to encourage the growth of the industry. This has centered on raising the awareness of currency as an asset class. The Foreign Exchange Institutional Sales team has spent time and resources informing its clients on the merits of such investments. "We've championed that because the foreign exchange market is scalable unlike any other asset, and returns are not correlated with alternative investments," Rodman said.

The group has created a learning environment that focuses on serving the client. For example, when the group started, it focused on executing transactions rather than providing clients with informed recommendations and strategies. "We had a single point of contact at the lowest end of the client rung," Rodman noted. "By focusing the way we have now, we can be meaningful all the way up to the chief investment officer of the organization."

Members of the sales team work to create an environment of respect for one another, focus, and fun. They also understand that there are several ways to reach a goal. "There is room for diversification of style and approach," Rodman said.

Because of the fast pace and intensity in the trading room, team members sometimes make mistakes. The workgroup supports learning from those mistakes. Brian Tracy, an associate with the group, noted, "They tell you what you did wrong, in a nonabrasive way. Everyone here is looking for a team P&L. They want to see the whole group do well, not see one guy suffer. They help you figure out how you can do it better the next time."

## Value People

One of the most striking findings of our research is that hard work and high expectations do not differentiate high-performing workgroups. They are necessary, but not sufficient, for high performance. What made the high-performing workgroups stand out was that they linked respect for people with those two factors. If the members don't feel valued for their contributions, all the hard work and high expectations in the world will not be enough for the group to be high performing.

As I said in Chapter 2, there is a correlation between valuing people and your ability to increase revenues and profits. The best way to value people is to show respect by treating smart people as if they are smart people. You don't tell them how to do their job; you trust them to do it well. You seek input from people with different functional expertise and natural strengths.

Tom Mendoza, president of Network Appliance, a California-based enterprise network storage solutions company listed for two consecutive years on *Fortune* magazine's "100 Best Companies to Work For," put it like this:

"If you're going to hire the best and brightest—and trust me, we look for the smartest people on earth and we have a lot of them—we want to give them enough information about what's really happening with the business. . . . We say 'this is working, that's not working; we're winning here, we're not winning here,' so that they can help you figure your way through this."

Mendoza tells people what he wants to accomplish, not how to accomplish it. He said he tells employees, " 'Look, I want to go to Pittsburgh.' I don't say 'here's the route you take' . . . [I tell them] 'I want you to figure out the most effective way . . . and here's the main thing I want you to do, I want you to get there fast.' "

Showing respect doesn't mean people can't push back, argue, or advocate strongly for their point of view. (There are ways to do that effectively, which I will discuss in Chapter 4.) Nor is it about being nice. In an environment where people respect each other's brainpower, there can be a lot of spirited disagreement. Coworkers may or may not like each other. But they value the contribution each person makes to the workgroup.

Tom Trueblood, a member of the Green Diesel Technology team, said that "this is a team where there are no holds barred. We really don't pull any punches—we're brutally honest with each other. We kid each other like crazy." But at the same time, he said, "There's a tremendous amount of respect that everyone on the team has for each member. We really listen to each other; we challenge each other."

Barbara Tinsley had twenty-eight years of legal experience when she joined Cendian, an Atlanta-based subsidiary of Eastman Chemical. She was immediately given a high-level project that typically would require sign-off by the general counsel. When it came time for him to approve the contract, he said, " 'If you're comfortable with it, you've got my approval,' " Tinsley recalled. "It made me feel empowered. . . . At Cendian everyone is treated with respect."

For Todd Musgrove, director of Professional Services at VA Software, respect means recognizing that his team members "are the technical experts and have the understanding of what the customer situation is." The California-based company provides tools to software developers to create new applications. Musgrove reminds team members that "they're empowered to make a decision, think about what's best for the customer, share this with the rest of the team, get input, and execute on that."

It is astounding how many smart, well-educated, and well-paid people are underutilized by their companies. And because their companies don't take full advantage of their skills and brainpower, they feel unappreciated. One of the study participants, a controller for a Midwest commercial printing company, summed up the feelings of many respondents. He said that quarterly profits improved about $1.5 million from the prior year, but that still wasn't enough.

"We've had a huge turnaround, yet some of the pressure coming from our executive group is just as strong or stronger," he said. "It's almost just not good enough to win the football game; you've got to have the most first downs, you've got to have the fewest penalties, you've got to not fumble the ball, it's like you've got to be almost perfect on all areas."

The same frustration is expressed by students in Professor Harry Davis's Business Policy course at the University of Chicago Graduate School of Business. Most of Davis's students work for major corporations. Excerpts from class papers they wrote about their work experience demonstrate their disappointment: "I'm bored." "Favoritism is rampant." "There's no room to grow in this organization." "I feel excluded." "I'm watched like a child." "I'm doing repetitive, unchallenging work."

People who feel this way cannot do their best work. Although they have the intelligence and the desire, their emotions get in the way of high performance. These emotions are reflected in their behavior—they can't concentrate, they work slower, they get sick.

What happens when people who are seen as underperformers are put in a workgroup in which their efforts are highly valued? That's exactly what happened at International Truck and Engine, and the results were remarkable.

The Green Diesel Technology team needed someone who could work on creating a retrofit kit, an important part of its strategy. A long-time employee (let's call him Ted) was asked to join the team. Ted seemed to be past his prime and was not considered a valuable player by the company.

Nevertheless, the team was so grateful to have him that they treated him like he was the messiah, said attorney Michele Smith, one of the members. "It was like 'hallelujah!' when he came in." Ted felt validated to be given such an important assignment. He threw himself into it, working night and day to get the project done.

"He was out there selling, finding out what to do. And [he went] on these demonstrations and worked with the dealers, the real nuts and bolts stuff of selling. We're a bunch of grand pooh-bahs in Public Affairs and things like that, and he's out there hitting the street," said Smith. The retrofit project turned into a $7 million piece of business for the company, and its single biggest area of growth. "It rejuvenated his career," according to Smith—all because he was treated with respect.

## Optimize Critical Thinking

Critical thinking involves analyzing information, drawing logical conclusions, and determining how to use the information to achieve the group's goals. To think critically, people have to get their emotions out of the way. They have to see congruity between leaders' words and their actions, and between the values that are preached and the values that are lived. They need to believe that the company does not withhold important information necessary to do their jobs. In this environment, people can stay focused. Without it, the incongruity between words and actions prompts an emotional response that distracts people from doing their best work. They spend more time keeping track of the contradictions than they do figuring out ways to make money for the company.

Our study demonstrated that one of the biggest differentiators between high-performing and nonperforming workgroups is the ability of the high-performing groups to optimize critical thinking. One of the study's most surprising findings is that for this to happen, the leader must protect the workgroup from the rest of the organization.

We asked those in high-performing groups to rate the applicability of the following statement to their workgroup on a scale of 0 to 10: "Our group leader protects us from the larger company so we can do our work." Respondents gave this statement a score of 7.0. It also was among the strongest differentiators between high-performing and nonperforming groups. Particularly interesting is that leaders rate the statement even higher than the study population at large. Taken together, the implication of these findings is that protection by the group leader is a necessary condition of high performance.

The leader protects the group in different ways. The protection can be positive, as when the leader goes to bat for the budget, lobbies for personnel or equipment, or gets the rules changed so that the group can operate with more flexibility. The formal leader of the Green Diesel Technology team, for example, persuaded top management to hire two key people who now work on the team.

"I work in a kind of old-line company where to ask for 'head count' is tantamount to death. You never want to ask for head count," according to Michele Smith. "The general counsel got permission to get those people hired. I don't know how he sold it."

Bobby Soules, a former facilities manager for SBC Communications, used a technique he calls "the hammer" in advocating for his workgroup. He took careful notes at meetings with upper managers, paying particular attention to their language in discussing organizational goals and issues. When seeking the support of these individuals, Soules "dropped the hammer," incorporating their language into his presentation. In this way, he was more likely to gain their support.

As a former finance director, Stephen Harvey, director of People and Culture at Microsoft UK, protects his human resources staff by teaching them to pay attention to the numbers and put a business spin on what they are trying to achieve. In that way they are more valuable to their internal customers and less likely to be "treated as pure overhead."

The other kind of protection occurs when the leader shields the group from company interference. That may involve absorbing criticism from others in the organization. Sometimes, protecting the group might simply involve looking the other way when a valuable member needs to work different hours than those permitted by the company. It may mean bending corporate rules or ignoring policies that the leader perceives are getting in the way of the group's performance.

Good leaders are tuned in to the organization and know which rules they can break and which they can't. They know that it is never permissible to break the law or violate ethics policies.

Ted Legasey, chief operating officer of SRA International, a Virginia-based information technology company, urges his managers to use common sense, while obeying the law. In one situation, a nonexempt employee asked at a meeting if she could work nine hours one day and seven hours the next, rather than eight each day. Legasey explained that the law requires paying overtime if she works nine hours. But then he added, "Now let's put common sense on top of that. If the right thing to do is for her to work nine hours one day and seven hours the next day, we pay her the one hour overtime. . . . Do what's right in the situation." SRA International was on *Fortune*'s list of "100 Best Places to Work For" in America for five years in a row.

One leader of a high-performing workgroup, a plant manager for a public company with $2 billion in annual sales, took a bold step to protect the workers at her plant from what she felt was an unfair company policy. The company's "gain sharing" program provided for workers to split a sum of money based on performance improvements during the year. However, the plant manager felt the program had a major flaw: It rewarded some people who played no role in making the improvements.

She told us, "The first year I uncovered this [I thought] 'Wow, this is wrong.' There was somebody in our Japan office getting part of the gain sharing from my plant in Indiana. And I said, 'No, no, no, what does this guy have to do with what we're doing here?' "

The plant manager already had credibility in the company because under her watch the plant reduced the number of defects in products sent to customers from more than one thousand parts per million to thirteen, without increasing manufacturing costs. The industry standard is fifteen parts per million.

After trying for two years to get the company to change its policy on how the money was awarded, she took matters into her own hands. She wrote a letter to everyone who got a payout but didn't contribute to the plant's results to say that as of a certain date they would no longer receive the payout. In her monthly report to executives, as well in an e-mail, she said that unless she was instructed otherwise, she was going to change the policy. She got no response. "My job is to protect the people who did earn [the money]. And so, I changed it," she said.

Top executives later called to question what she had done, but at that point all they could do was agree to use corporate funds to pay the people who had been cut off, rather than the funds set aside for the plant. She also changed the system—which had provided for smaller payouts each successful year—to reward continued high performance.

"This year ended on a good note because the people got what they deserved, and going forward, I fixed a broken system so this wouldn't happen to them again," she said.

In this case, the plant manager protected the financial interests of her workgroup at some risk to herself. She felt good about what she did, and the results were positive. However, there is a downside when the leader has to continually protect a high-performing group from company interference. When this occurs, the company is paying a talented individual to spend valuable time thinking of ways to get around the interference, rather than using that creativity to create a new product, market, or service. The result is wasted time, money, and energy.

Company interference often takes the form of incongruity between words and actions, or between the values that are espoused and the business decisions that are made. For example, the company professes to care about its people, but does nothing to show appreciation. The company says that it wants the best thinking from employees, but then withholds the information they need to do that thinking. The company says it values performance, but doesn't pay what people are worth. The company says it values empowerment, but tells people precisely what to do and how to do it. When the leader is forced to protect the group from these inconsistencies, or must try to explain them, the toll is high.

When there is too much interference, the workgroup develops an "us versus them" mentality. The members begin to think that they are better than the rest of the company, and they go undercover, trying to get results despite the interference. They become a secret society, unwilling to share their successful strategies with anyone. At the same time, the leader becomes so frustrated that he starts to bad-mouth the company to senior managers, who begin to perceive him as a complainer, rather than someone who has constructive ideas. They only put up with him because his group is still getting results.

These leaders stay with the company for a long time, primarily because they are loyal to their group. But one day a recruiter calls, and their frustration has become so overwhelming that they leave the company. In the exit interview, they explain that they are leaving for more money and a better job. Management takes that at face value, never becoming aware of the interference or learning from what occurred. The protection goes away, and the group's performance often declines over time.

There are numerous examples of conflicts between words and actions in corporate America. One study participant, whom we'll call Bill—an employee of one of the largest computer manufacturers in the world—told us about a manager who liked to have "round table time" during which anyone could speak. At one meeting soon after he started, Bill took the invitation at face value and asked why the business unit would initiate a big program, under-staff it, and then "sell" it as if it were "widely, hugely successful when it's really not."

Rather than being rewarded for having the courage to question the leader, Bill was written up for insubordination. "Obviously [from then on] it was, 'everything's great, [I have] nothing to add.' I felt like I was hired on for a good reason, like I had something to offer. Now the thing that I had to offer I don't have anymore."

Bill said that this was not an isolated incident. Whenever people expressed an opinion that was contrary to—or appeared to be contrary to—the "go team go" mind-set of the group, they were disciplined.

When the workgroup lives the values it espouses—and especially when that philosophy comes from the top—the results are impressive. CEO Paul Spiegelman and his brothers started the Texas-based Beryl Companies in 1985 as an emergency response center for elderly people. The business began in a rented room with a cot and a telephone. Today the privately owned company, which provides referrals and information about health-care resources, employs 225 people and has about $15 million in annual sales.

"The culture at Beryl begins at top management and flows through to all their managers and employees," one employee said. In 2003, the company was named one of the top ten mid-size places to work in the Dallas/Fort Worth market by the *Dallas Business Journal*.

The business has had three values from the start:

passion for customer service, always doing the right thing, and never sacrificing quality. "The amazing thing is . . . that I could go down right now to the call center floor and say 'tell me the three values' and the vast majority of people would right off the top of their heads tell me what they are," said Spiegelman. "Those are the things that no matter what business we're in will always be with us. They don't change," he said.

Living the values begins with hiring employees who have compassion and a desire to help others, and extends to all of the company's decision making. "[The values] make it so much easier to do business," Spiegelman said. For example, the company will turn down a potentially lucrative new business opportunity if it believes its ability to provide quality service will be compromised.

"I think we all do really try to 'do the right thing' day in and day out, making coworkers feel comfortable trusting their management," a Beryl employee said.

"For us to maintain our values and build a family of coworkers that share those values, we had to have control of our own destiny," Spiegelman said. "And that may mean being a smaller company than we could otherwise have been."

## Seize Opportunities

If your company is like most, you put a lot of time and effort into strategic planning. For your business to grow, you need to create a plan and measure your progress against your goals. However, our study found that doing these things is necessary but not sufficient: Both high-performing and nonperforming workgroups make plans and measure progress. What distinguishes the high-performing groups is that they create a learning environment in which people can seize opportunities—take risks, generate new ideas, and make mistakes.

According to Blair Miller, an internationally known expert on human creativity and innovation, the critical issue is whether people are rewarded for learning or "nailed for it." When results are not as good as expected, "we need to, in a deliberate way, figure out what occurred, what we are going to learn, and what to do differently next time." Without this, Miller said, "you can have all the slogans you want, but you're not going to have risk taking."

Avery Dennison, a global office products company, encourages learning, and one result is higher revenue. The company creates cross-functional teams that have one hundred days to produce a new product, service, or market. "The learning piece is to identify what you know, what you don't know, and how to get the information you need to deliver on the goal," said Stella Estevez, vice president of Leadership and Organization Development.

One team's project was to set up a supply chain to distribute three new product categories and sell an order from one of them. After one hundred days, the team had created the supply chain and sold products from all three of the product lines; in 2003, sales on these reached $1.2 million. The team is continuing to work together on new projects. "You have some core members there but you always have different people on the periphery that are contributing and getting that experience," said Tom Van Dessel, director of Growth for the Specialty Tape Division.

A company that permits risk taking also must tolerate mistakes. Tom Mendoza, president of Network Appliance, tells the story of an incident that occurred early in the company's history that helped reinforce a culture of risk taking. The company's disk drive supplier put the entire industry on allocation, meaning the supply would be severely limited. "The only alternative was to make a one-time, large bulk buy," Mendoza said. NetApp purchased 2,000 drives at a premium price. Soon after the company took delivery of the product, the supplier took NetApp off allocation. "We now were faced with the issue of far too many drives, bought at a high price, and a market surplus, which meant the same drives were now available for far less from other suppliers.

"We sent Sales and Marketing executives off, they reconstructed how they were going to package it, and we sold our way out of it," Mendoza recalled. "The thing that struck me is that no one ever asked 'who did it?' And the reason it was never asked, is that it was done for the right reason."

NetApp encourages risk taking by publicly recognizing people who make an extraordinary effort, regardless of the results. "If you go attack [the problem] with passionate integrity and use every bit of ingenuity you have and you don't succeed, I will take care of you. Not only won't you get hurt, I'm going to make sure something good happens to you for making that effort," Mendoza said.

Companies that foster a learning environment have the ability to turn problems into opportunities. NetApp, which in fiscal year 2003 had about $900 million in annual sales, was flying high in early 2001 when management realized that the deepening recession required a radical change in strategy. At that time NetApp was the third fastest-growing company in the United States; the company generated twenty-one consecutive quarters with more than 70 percent year-over-year revenue growth, from its IPO in November 1995 to January 2001.

When the recession hit, technology customers, which represented 70 percent of the company's revenue, drastically cut back on their spending. NetApp anticipated that it could not continue to rely on its core revenue base and also recognized that the recession opened up a tremendous opportunity to sell to nontechnology companies. The company hadn't had much success selling to these firms during the boom years when price wasn't an issue.

In fact, the CIO of one major New York brokerage firm told Mendoza, "You'll never sell me or anyone else on Wall Street if your value proposition is that you can do what the other guys do as well or better for a lot less money. What we have already works. Why would we look to change it? There's no pain point." After the brokerage firm's budget went down 20 percent a year for two years, it felt the pain.

"That firm bought over $15 million of our product in two years," Mendoza said.

As a result of the recession, NetApp's sales to technology companies dropped from $700 million to $250 million in one year. "We could have gotten annihilated," Mendoza said. "But we switched the company on a dime. We changed the messaging of the company in twenty-four hours."

Rather than emphasizing its technology and speed, Net-App decided to focus on the business solutions that customers were likely to invest in during the recession. "They all had a desperate problem; they had to do more with less. Then 9/11 happened," Mendoza said. The terrorist attack reinforced the need for reliable data backup and recovery systems at a lower cost, and NetApp jumped at the opportunity.

The company decided to fund four things that it bet were the most important to customers: data consolidation, which would reduce spending on service contracts; data recovery from disk, rather than tape; a disaster recovery system that uses the same product utilized for storage; and a single solution to back up both centralized and distributed data.

The new strategy required NetApp to replace about 40 percent of its sales force over two years. Whereas before the sales staff was selling to other technology people in a boom time, now "we had to figure out the problem, tell [the customer] how we could save them money and then get them to think about buying when they weren't ready to buy. It's a different skill set," Mendoza said.

Ironically, the recession reinvigorated NetApp, as well as Tom Mendoza personally. "I almost started losing interest when it kept going so well because I figured anybody could do this. But here's something else that struck me immediately. The recession was our opportunity to take share big time from the incumbents." The company's ability to change focus paid off. "Network Appliance was able to overcome the loss of technology revenue with enterprise wins; it lost only 20 percent in total revenue, and kept its business model intact," Mendoza said.

## Field of Dreams

BKR Rosenbergs, an accounting firm in Australia, is an example. So is Microsoft UK. And Macquarie Capital Partners, a real estate investment-banking boutique firm based in Chicago. They built an environment on a foundation of respect, and people have come.

In Melbourne, Australia, Harry Rosenberg's firm, BKR Rosenbergs, has a policy that team members come first. The firm's TLC (Team Lifestyle and Care) policy permeates every aspect of the business. The company fosters a culture in which team members' needs are met, which can mean providing training, rewarding people for performance, recognizing achievement, or supporting them in their personal lives.

"The more that's put into the team members in terms

of . . . creating an environment within which they're happy to be working, the more I get back. You can't expect to get a lot if you don't give a lot. It's very simple," Rosenberg said. While it's normally difficult to hire good accountants with two to five years of experience, Rosenberg's firm has no problem attracting top talent. When people talk about why they joined the firm, they say "it's because of the TLC program," he added.

Rosenberg took a risk when he instituted the program. He could have been perceived as "someone who isn't tough, who isn't ruthless. . . . The risk was to come out formally and enunciate such a culture—put it into words," he said. Clearly, it was a risk worth taking: Accountants fight for the chance to work at BKR Rosenbergs.

Macquarie Capital Partners was deliberately created to be an investment bank that rivals any on Wall Street for talent and commitment, but it is also a place where people love to go to work. "We want to do the very intellectually stimulating work of investment bankers, but in a different environment," explained managing principal Don Suter. People came to Macquarie from JPMorgan Chase, Morgan Stanley, Merrill Lynch, Citigroup, and other top firms because they were attracted by the company's value proposition.

For example, there are no superstars at Macquarie. Everyone has the same size work space. Associates and above have an ownership stake after a few years with the company. People are strongly discouraged from working on weekends. Macquarie's investment bankers could work anywhere. "They all get offers but they don't leave," Suter said. "They are attracted by the culture, lack of bureaucracy, and the ability to have an immediate impact on transactions."

To earn the right to work at a high-performing company, knowledge workers need to carry their weight. "You have to make sure that you can identify employees who are not performing," said Andrew Tucker, partner of New York–based investment services firm Brown Brothers Harriman and chairman of its European subsidiaries. "Not only are they costing you money but they are demoralizing workers around them who say, 'Why should I work as hard as I do when this person is not performing?'"

People also need to feel that their work matters—whether they work on an assembly line or own the company. Shell UK Chairman Clive Mather, referring to his executive team, put it well. "I do think people feel that what they're doing matters. . . . At the end of the day, whatever the challenges are—they are worth it. I don't wake up in the morning and think, 'How are we going to get through this day?' I wake up and think, 'What a privilege to have this opportunity.' I am proud of what we are trying to do."

Stephen Harvey, director of People and Culture at Microsoft UK, noted that when people at his company come to work, "they have the chance to do what they do best every day. So when a headhunter calls they say, 'Why would I want to work anywhere else?'" According to the *Sunday*

*Times* (London), Microsoft UK is the best company to work for in Britain. It is also the most successful revenue-producing division in Microsoft.

If people believe they can make a difference, they will come. If they are given the opportunity to do their jobs well, they will stay. Most importantly, if you build the right environment, they will perform. However, our research shows that even high-performing workgroups can do better. By practicing the principles described in Chapters 4 and 5, your company will not only become a talent magnet, it will achieve even more powerful results.

## Key Points

To sustain profitable growth, you need to create an environment where people feel valued, can do their best thinking, and have the latitude to seize opportunities as they arise.

- Value people: The best way to show respect is to treat smart people as if they are smart people. Showing respect doesn't mean people can't push back, argue, or advocate strongly for their point of view. Nor is it about being nice.
- Optimize critical thinking: To think critically, people have to get their emotions out of the way. They have to see congruity between leaders' words and their actions, and between the values that are preached and the values that are lived. They need to believe that the company does not withhold important information necessary to do their jobs.
- Seize opportunities: To drive high performance, companies need an environment where people have the latitude to seize opportunities as they arise.
- Build it and they will come: If people believe they can make a difference, they will come. If they are given the opportunity to do their jobs well, they will stay. Most importantly, if you build the right environment, they will perform.

## Unexpected Findings

- Hard work and high expectations do not differentiate high-performing workgroups. What made the high-performing workgroups stand out was that they linked respect for people with those two factors.

- In high-performing workgroups, the leader protects the workgroup from the rest of the organization.

- For your business to grow, you need to create a plan and measure your progress against goals. However, our study found that both high-performing and nonperforming workgroups make plans and measure progress. What distinguishes the high-performing groups is that they create a learning environment in which people can take risks, generate new ideas, make mistakes, and learn from them.

# CHAPTER 4

# Room to Grow

The fastest, most effective way to achieve profitable growth is to increase the performance of your company's best workgroups. Even your highest-performing business units have the capacity to do better.

How do you identify these high-performing groups? These are the groups that get financial results, based on accepted metrics in your company such as unit profitability, EBITDA, and ROI. They introduce new products, services, markets, or processes. And, they foster an environment built on valuing people, optimizing critical thinking, and seizing opportunities. Based on these factors, you can create an instrument that pinpoints strengths and weaknesses within each group. (See Results the Right Way: The Environment of High-Performing Workgroups, next page.)

The Hudson Highland Center for High Performance also has developed a proprietary Web-enabled survey that allows you to benchmark your workgroups against global performance standards. The instrument, Hudson Highland PerformancePeak, isolates the behaviors that drive high performance and weights them based on the degree of differentiation between high-performing and nonperforming workgroups.

If the high-performing workgroups you identify are like those in our study, they too have room to grow. In the study, we asked survey participants to rate their workgroups from

*Results the Right Way:*
*The Environment of High-Performing Workgroups*

Here are some of the factors that define high-performing workgroups:

- Learn what customers want
- Continually look for ways to be more efficient
- Allow people to take risks
- Measure progress against goals
- Make members feel valued
- Adapt quickly to changes in the environment
- Provide nonfinancial recognition for high performance
- See mistakes as opportunities to learn
- Make use of the highest and best talents of employees
- Invest in training and upgrading of skills

## Getting Results the Right Way: Room to Grow

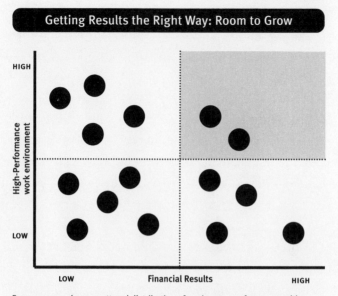

Every company has a scattered distribution of workgroup performance, with groups represented in each quadrant. Start by finding your high-performing workgroups.

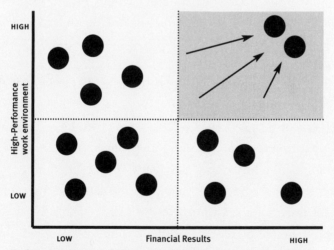

The fastest, easiest way to increase organizational performance is by helping the already high-performing workgroups get even better. In the global study, even the highest-performing groups scored only 7.8 out of 10.

o to 10 on a series of performance measures. On average, those who belonged to high-performing workgroups rated their group's performance at 7.0 and scored no measure higher than 7.8.

In this chapter, you will find examples of top workgroups that have increased their performance, as well as specific models that you can use to improve performance in your own company. I will describe both the environment necessary for people to freely exchange information and honest opinions and the communication processes utilized by high-performing organizations. When these components come together, the likelihood that workgroups will achieve high performance increases exponentially.

Some high-performing groups take responsibility for their own improvement. They seek out ideas from within the group or draw on others in the company. In other cases, the company steps in to try to further accelerate the performance of these groups.

The Client Implementation team at Cendian, a chemical and plastics logistics company, increased its already high performance by seeking broader input from the rest of the company. "Early on, we were doing 'one-off' [customized] solutions for clients that didn't fit with the general idea of where we wanted to go as a company," recalled the director of Client Implementation. However, more recently when the implementation group needed to modify its product offering for a particular client, it called together a cross-functional team from various areas of the company, including product management, finance, supplier platforms, and technology, to address the problem.

By reaching out to other parts of the company, the Client Implementation team solved the client's problem, and at the same time grew the business base by adding to the company's product offerings. The client also is going to open doors to other clients in its segment of the industry. The project represented $80 million to $100 million in volume for Cendian. The customer is expected to save about $600,000 on the initial implementation.

The Cendian workgroup improved its own performance. However, there are times when senior leadership needs to step in to remove obstacles to high performance that it inadvertently put in the way. I have never met a senior leadership group that plotted to deliberately reduce the performance of the organization. However, we know from our research that these barriers are there and that leaders of high-performing groups protect their groups from them. The best way around this is for senior leaders to step in to remove the interference they have unintentionally created.

That's what happened at a large division of a major energy company. Watching its stock price tumble and performance targets go unmet, the division's leaders took some bold steps to try to return the company to its former position at the top of the industry. They determined that there were so many cultural factors inhibiting progress—including a burdensome bureaucracy—that there wasn't time to fix them all. Instead, they decided to focus on removing the biggest obstacles to performance, breaking rules if necessary.

The executives held a high-level leadership conference during which the division's executive vice president admitted that he had made mistakes. He also acknowledged that "yes, we are a bureaucracy—there is no escaping that. But guess what, team: so is every other competitor out there—and they're beating the pants off of us."

By making these statements the executive cleared the way for others to speak the unspeakable and to have a meaningful discussion about the impact of these issues on the company's bottom line. The meeting also sent a clear signal that things were going to be different going forward. Among the commitments the executive made was to cut the number of required financial reports in half.

The company also initiated a challenge to each of ten leadership teams to identify roadblocks to success and develop specific methods for eliminating them. At the leadership conference, the teams came up with goals they could implement immediately, including reducing the number of technology projects funded from 125 to 30. One participant pointed out, "Leadership isn't rocket science, it's committing to letting your people go out and do what it takes."

Within three months, the initiatives that began at the meeting had contributed millions of dollars to the company's bottom line. Although the results were impressive, it was too little, too late: Less than six months after the leadership conference, the once-proud company was swallowed up by a competitor.

Lion-Nathan, the second largest brewer in Australia, also instituted a process from the top to reverse a troubling decline in performance. In this case, the company came out stronger than ever.

In the mid-1990s, Lion-Nathan's sales were headed downward. "We came to the conclusion that [the solution] was all about making sure we had the right culture and the right leaders to allow our people to deliver the results we wanted," said John Perez, Culture and Change leader for the brewer. "Leadership to us equals coaching. So [the initiative] was around how do we develop leaders who then allow teams to be able to deliver great results."

The company put in place an in-house, three-day program in which the members of each workgroup get feedback about their styles and behaviors. They receive intensive coaching on ways to improve their interpersonal relationships and how they work together as a team. Participants also work on understanding obstacles that prevent the group from doing its best work.

"We give people . . . feedback on how they can make the environment the right environment to allow high performance," Perez said. In addition, each member of the team gets individual feedback, and gives the other members input on how their behavior affects the group.

Every two years the company does a culture survey on the organization as a whole and on each of the workgroups.

Each workgroup leader presents the results to the rest of the team, which prepares an action plan to address the issues "that are stopping our culture from being the way we want it to be," Perez said.

Since Lion-Nathan has used the same tool for the last eight years, it has been able to document the improvement in its work environment. Business performance also continues to improve. From 2000 to 2003, annual sales rose 41 percent from $878 million to $1.2 billion (in U.S. dollars). During the same period, net income increased from $2 million to $122 million, according to Hoover's, an online business research tool.

## The Leader's Role

To sustain high performance, you need your workgroups to get results the right way. The leader has a part to play, but he or she is not the linchpin of the environment. "Leadership is not something that is inside of you or me; leadership is in the environments that we create," according to Linda Ginzel, clinical professor of managerial psychology at the University of Chicago Graduate School of Business.

Nor is there a single personality or style that defines an effective leader. As Lion-Nathan recognized, the leader of a high-performing workgroup makes sure that the right environment can flourish. "We have leaders in our business now who . . . take responsibility for what they do in setting the right environment for their teams," said Perez.

I have seen leaders whose styles could not be more different foster high performance in their groups. However, they all understand the importance of creating an environment in which people can do their best work. While leaders are different, the environments that foster high performance are remarkably similar.

The Product Development group of a large tobacco company offers a good example of how leaders with different styles can be effective, as long as they don't tamper with a successful environment. A manager in the group (I'll call him Doug Barry) has worked under four vice presidents. The first three had very different approaches. One was a "a fine man, interested in people, interested in who you were, knew the business up and down, always there to lend a hand. He would walk down the halls just to see what you were . . . working on and sit down and chat with you," Barry said.

The next VP was a "great guy," but "he didn't want to know anything. He just wanted to be left alone to do his work." VP number three "did his own thing" and didn't worry about what anyone else did. Under all of these vice presidents, Barry's group was relatively autonomous and successful.

Then the fourth head of research and development, who was from a different industry, came in and decided to make a lot of changes. His motives were good: He wanted to develop the people in the group and cut costs. He reorganized, increasing the number of directors and managers from ten to twenty. "He wonders why our work went down. He just took ten good R&D folks out of the workforce and made them managers," said Barry.

The VP cut the number of Barry's direct reports from fourteen to five, and at the time of our interview, he was about to further split up the group. His approach is, "I want to know everything, I want to be in the middle of everything, I want you to tell everything to me and I even want you to ask permission for everything. What a difference!" said Barry.

Many group members perceive the VP to be more concerned about himself than about their interests. "Nobody trusts him as far as we can throw him. Period. He's generally considered to be a backstabber and I've had several instances where he's turned around on me in midstream and made me look bad. He'll tell me one thing and in a meeting [say] something else; he'll do a 180 on you."

The first three executives, although they had different styles and different personalities, understood that the environment of the group allowed people to perform. "They were all old tobacco guys. They had been in the industry for years, they knew how it worked, they knew how small R&D organizations functioned," said Barry. "They trusted us and they left us alone."

While the new leader may have come in with the best intentions in the world, he killed the group's esprit de corps. "Morale is awful here. I've been here a long time and I've never seen it this bad . . . it's gotten into a management nightmare, which has just bogged down the work processes. His reorganization just destroyed the ambition of so many people," Barry commented. The vice president tampered with the environment that made it all work. The situation has not yet taken its toll on the bottom line, but Barry is sure that it will. It has certainly taken its toll on Barry—he is thinking about retiring three years earlier than he originally planned.

## Know Yourself

The single most important quality that leaders must have to foster a high-performing environment is honesty about themselves. They need to be clear about what they bring to the table—their own strengths and weaknesses. This paves the way for leaders to make sure that their workgroup includes people who have the skills they lack. They can't, and don't need to, have all the skills themselves. If the leader is not able to show empathy, for example, she doesn't have to go to a training program. She should hire someone who is empathetic to help her.

"One of the other things we tell our leaders is 'you've got to know yourself first,' " said Ted Legasey, chief operating officer of SRA International, an information technology services company that made *Fortune*'s "100 Best Companies to Work For" in America list for five years straight. "You've got to know what your strengths are, you've got to know your weaknesses so that you can either work on improving those weaknesses or you have some jumper wires that you can put around the weak parts that you have and empower other people to do things that you're not particularly good at."

Professor Harry Davis of the University of Chicago Graduate School of Business notes that leaders today need qualities that have not necessarily been associated with leadership in the past, such as patience and the ability to listen. Particularly important is the willingness of leaders to say "I don't know the answer," Davis said. "What we need are people who can be more and more authentic in terms of bringing all that they have to bear, and getting other people in the organization to bring all of who they are to their work."

While leadership is important, many high-performing workgroups are too leader-dependent. When a strong leader leaves, the environment that fosters high performance usually goes away too. It is possible that the next leader will come in and leave the environment alone, but that is unusual. Conversely, senior leaders may think that if a workgroup has a strong leader, they can take away resources and set unrealistic deadlines and somehow the group will prevail.

Companies encourage leader-dependence when they evaluate leaders only on their individual competency. It's understandable that they do this because, in our society, we focus on individual performance. We work to get an A grade, be accepted to the university, beat out someone else to get the job. We present the Heisman Trophy and the Cy Young Award to individuals who play team sports.

"Decades of research have shown that we focus on the person and not the situational causes of behavior," pointed out social psychologist Linda Ginzel. "We vastly underestimate the role of situations or factors outside the person. Why does this matter? When we are wrong, we're making a mistake about what caused certain outcomes, and this makes it difficult to learn from the past and difficult to improve in the future. But more importantly, we are ignoring the only thing that we can actually change—the environment."

In addition to providing 360-degree feedback on individuals for their own professional development, companies need to evaluate the environment of their workgroups. This evaluation must be based on observable behaviors, not attitudes or opinions. Does the group respect different points of view? Is it willing to take risks? Does it live the values it espouses? Does it recognize and celebrate accomplishments? These are some of the behaviors that our study correlates with making money for the company. They are the responsibility of the whole group, and the group should be rewarded for them.

As a result of a recent culture survey, brewer Lion-Nathan determined that one team had a weak leader. "The leader brought some things to the environment, but not others," explained Ken Davis, Group Business Services director at the company. "We didn't replace the leader, we looked at how the group could complement the leader, how the team members could modify their styles," Davis said.

At Macquarie Capital Partners, everyone in the company feels responsible for maintaining the environment. "We're very protective of the people we bring into this firm because we all know we've got something unique here in terms of the culture and how people work with each other, and we want to maintain that," said Christopher Vallace, a principal at the Chicago-based investment bank. People want to work at Macquarie because it's different from the typical Wall Street investment bank, even though it might mean making less money in the short term.

Everyone in the firm spends time with a potential new hire to determine whether the person is a good fit. "Do they have these stereotypical Wall Street attributes that we all wanted to get away from or do they share a lot of the values that we do? If it's the former, regardless of how bright they are we don't even consider them," Vallace said.

## Offering Amnesty

In every company, certain subjects are only discussed behind closed doors. The problem is that often these "unspeakable" statements are the most important ones for leaders to hear and for the workgroup to tackle. They need to be said out loud, not at the "meeting after the meeting."

The subjects people are most afraid to talk about are those that leaders most need to address.

Often workers are so sure their leaders won't listen if they tell the truth that they don't even try. Some fear that they will be ostracized or even fired. "Managers with a lot of authority need to be especially careful not to punish people, explicitly or implicitly, for speaking out, particularly on issues that may be difficult for the organization to deal with," noted a May 2003 article in the *Harvard Business Review*.

Before your company can improve its high-performing workgroups—and thus improve its overall performance—it needs to bring taboo subjects into the light. There are steps companies can take to encourage workers to speak the unspeakable. The first is to invite representatives of your high-performing workgroups to a tell-all meeting with the CEO and other members of the senior leadership team.

At this meeting, leaders must acknowledge that they are inadvertently creating barriers to high performance, and offer amnesty for telling the truth. They'll promise that no one will be fired, no one's budget is going to be taken away, no one is going to be punished. For amnesty to work, it has to be offered in public. That is the best way to ensure that the promises will be kept. I also recommend that organizations hire an outside facilitator whose job is to ensure that the leaders keep to the subject, are specific, and confront uncomfortable issues head on. The facilitator will also help the leaders by giving them a second chance when they get defensive or don't adequately answer the question.

At one such meeting, during which participants were offered amnesty, a manager got up and said that he had been unable to get a senior leader, whom he named, to meet with government officials in Asia to discuss a very large business deal. The manager noted that presidents and chairmen from the company's competitors in the region had met with the officials, but his leaders "couldn't be bothered." He added, "Our top leadership isn't leading, it's managing."

Although he felt like he had taken his life into his hands when he told the truth, later that evening he was presented with an award for having the courage to speak up. When he came to the podium, he said that he had called his wife earlier and told her he was going to be fired. Instead, he got an award and a standing ovation. By publicly honoring him, the company sent a powerful message about the behavior it wanted to encourage.

For the tell-all meeting to be effective, you need respectful communication. Not surprisingly, this is the kind of communication that takes place in high-performing workgroups. Respectful communication allows brainpower to be engaged; it minimizes the emotions that stifle effective dialogue (see Respectful Communication on the next page).

The two most important rules in respectful communication are: Always assume good intent; and Identify the logic. If you assume that someone's motives for bringing up a particular idea or making a comment are in the best

*Respectful Communication*

The purpose of respectful communication is to keep the conversation on an intellectual level. Once emotions enter into the dialogue, thinking gets lost.

- **Assume positive intent:** Reverse any negative assumptions you may be making, e.g., "The person is stupid."
- **State your confusion:** Say, "I'm confused. Can you help me understand *why* your idea will ____?"
- **Identify the logic:** Keep asking why until you understand what's smart about the person's thinking. Don't give up too fast—you may inadvertently lose a brilliant idea.
- **Repeat back:** After you have identified the logic, repeat it back to ensure accuracy.
- **Identify the holes:** If you see a flaw in the person's thinking, identify any holes or dangers in the logic. "My concern is if we go that route, ____ might happen. Have you accounted for ____?" Either she will have thought of your concern and can address it to your satisfaction, or she has not accounted for it and will work with you to deal with it.

interests of the company—that they are not driven by an ulterior motive or self-interest—you are much more likely to find out what is smart about the idea. If you assume negative intent, you're likely to label the idea or the person: "That's a dumb idea;" or "She's stupid." But your job is not to label; it's to comprehend.

If you're not convinced that the idea is smart, you need to say that you are confused, and ask the person to explain the logic that led to his conclusion. Assume that if you fully understood his point, you would agree. Repeat it back to make sure you have it right. Ask questions. Stay with it until you grasp the logic.

If you don't practice respectful communication, you are in danger of missing a brilliant idea. In fact, if an idea seems strange to you, it may be because it is outside your realm of experience. This is likely to occur increasingly often in today's diverse, globalized economy. If you're not willing to delve into the idea, you might miss an important paradigm shift. One widely quoted example of a paradigm shift took place in the watchmaking industry in the 1960s. The quartz watch was invented in Switzerland and presented first to Swiss watch manufacturers, who rejected it because it had no moving parts and thus did not fit their conception of a watch. Texas Instruments saw the paradigm shift and brought the quartz watch to market. Between 1969 and 1980, the Swiss share of the watch market plummeted from 65 percent to less than 10 percent.

Of course it's possible that an idea is not smart and that

the person who presented it has gaps in his reasoning. If, after a process of respectful communication, you still think there is a gap in the logic, there probably is. But at that point, the other person is likely to see the gap too.

While the goal of respectful communication is to keep emotions at bay so that you can enhance brainpower, you can't ever totally eliminate emotions from the dialogue. Someone will say something that upsets you, and no matter how hard you try to assume positive intent, you won't be able to do it. At that point, you should get out of the room and calm down. Go talk to the one person who you can always count on to be on your side. Once you release the emotion, you can access your brain and solve the problem.

Disrespectful communication promotes the "gotcha" game. In this game, your goal is to find the hole in the other person's argument and prove that he is stupid and you are smart. When you attack his thinking, he is taken by surprise and begins to use emotional logic. He comes up with an explanation for why you think he is stupid. Usually it's because you're stupid. When this process occurs, brainpower gets lost. Although the words may be different, this is like a playground argument that no one wins.

Christopher Vallace, of Macquarie Capital Partners, has worked for firms at which people are very focused on getting individual credit for transactions that they participated in. "That creates a very selfish environment in which you're not only promoting a star system, but you've also got individuals [who are] doing things [so] they can look better than some of their peers," he said.

High-performing groups don't play gotcha. They communicate respectfully, and share ownership of solutions. What makes Macquarie different from other investment banks is how people approach their work, Vallace said. "The difference here is the collaborative nature of it. It's competitive but in a rewarding way to the firm, not in a rewarding way to an individual. We all kind of push each other in a good way."

One of the reasons the Green Diesel Technology team at International Truck and Engine has been so successful is that no idea is rejected out of hand, regardless of where it comes from. "We look at things from each other's point of view and are respectful of the talents of other people on the team," said Michele Smith, general counsel for the company's engine group. "One thing you never hear on our team is 'your opinion doesn't count because it's not your area.' That may be the strongest thing we have going for us," Smith added.

## Collaboration Model

In a tell-all meeting, and in many other situations, you are likely to identify complex problems that require collaborative thinking to solve. Companies use various collaboration models. I will describe one that I have found particularly effective in encouraging the flow of ideas. I first developed it when I was asked to facilitate a team-building session for the senior executive team of an entrepreneurial company that was growing rapidly. I have used it many times since, and the result is that people walk away highly committed to executing the outcome, because they participated in reaching it (see Collaboration Model on page 103).

When I walked into that team-building session, it felt like someone had just died. The team members had decided to purchase a Japanese company, but when they presented their case to their parent, a European holding company, they were turned down. They felt the acquisition would give them a competitive advantage and allow them to continue on their high growth curve. They also had invested a great deal of time, effort, and emotional energy in the plan, so they were very upset.

I allowed them to vent their emotions for an hour. I then asked them to list the assumptions they were making about why their plan was rejected. Here's what I heard: "Our parent company doesn't want to give up any control." "They don't trust us." "They are only thinking about the short term." "They don't respect our opinion." "They don't really know how to be competitive." "They used the wrong measures to evaluate the acquisition." On and on they went. If their negative assumptions were correct, they were also correct that the situation was hopeless. However, it was possible that their assumptions were wrong.

I went up to the board and reversed each statement, writing the words "What if?" in front of it. For example, I asked, "What if the parent company's leaders aren't controlling? What if they trust everybody in the room? What if they have a long-term view?" After I reversed all the assumptions, I asked the group, "If these new assumptions were true, how would you solve this problem?" As soon as I said this, people started sitting up straighter, and their brains began to work. A myriad of ideas came forth that were blocked before the exercise.

We then discussed the best way to convince the parent company to change its decision. What would be the most persuasive arguments? As in traditional brainstorming, the rule was that all ideas count. Don't cross any out, don't discuss them, just put them on the board. Don't stop when you get a good idea. One idea begat the next, and as the ideas flowed, they became richer and richer. Soon the group began to own the ideas—they no longer belonged to individuals.

We next took each idea and identified what was smart about it. A pattern emerged from all the ideas that allowed the group members to come together on a solution—the smartest way to convince the company to change its mind. They then selected the person who could present the case in a culturally sensitive way. Within three days of the meeting, the parent company reversed its decision.

*Practices of High-Performing Workgroups*

In more than seventy-five in-depth interviews conducted for this book, many people shared tactics that their workgroups use to drive high performance. Below are some of the practices.

1. **Red handle process:** The red handle process allows anyone in the workgroup to go to a preselected officer in the company who is not directly involved with the group, and raise a serious concern. The designated person rotates from year to year. The red handle is used only as a last resort, after the person has tried to resolve the problem with direct supervisors. This process is similar to the "circuit breaker" used by the Navy. Even the lowest-ranking person on the flight deck has the authority—and the obligation—to suspend flight operations immediately if he perceives a problem. But in this case, he doesn't need to go through the chain of command.

2. **Most Intelligent Failure award:** RSM McGladrey recommends that companies trying to develop a culture that rewards accountability and entrepreneurial behavior give this award. It goes to an individual who saw an opportunity; thoroughly researched it; created the environment, the team, the resources, and the conditions

necessary for the best chance at success; left no stone unturned; burned the midnight oil to get it done—and failed completely. Winners get a substantial cash price and a personal car wash from the CEO in the company parking lot.

3. **BIGDOG:** Michigan-based accounting firm Plante & Moran actively solicits new ideas through BIGDOG (Business Innovation Group Developing Operational Greatness), a committee of directors, associates, and staff members from throughout the firm. BIGDOG acknowledges every idea, and employees are eligible for gifts and cash prizes for submissions. BIGDOG holds an "idea sale" and awards cash prizes for the top three ideas. The "sale" is held during tax season, a time of intense contact with clients during which the best ideas emerge.

4. **Three things that will make a difference:** Network Appliance president Tom Mendoza asks new employees to come up with three things that they're going to do to make an impact on the company in their first six months and submit them to their boss. If one or two of those are rejected, they haven't wasted an ounce of energy, he says. "Activity is your enemy. What we want is impact. We ask, what are the two or three things that if you nail them, you'll have made a big impact?"

5. **Wow! cards:** One consumer products company encourages employees to send preformatted e-mails to col-

leagues, recognizing them for superior performance. The e-mail is copied to senior management. "It doesn't translate to a monetary award or any special privileges," said the survey respondent, but it's not overused, and people feel good when they receive it. In addition, the message goes in the individual's personal file, so it becomes a factor when review time rolls around.

6. **Word power:** The Midlands Development team at UNITE Group PLC uses a creative system to help manage internal dynamics. The team came up with a "rude word" that members use when they think someone is being especially annoying. They reasoned that the individual probably doesn't set out to irritate the others and may not realize he is coming across as annoying. Speaking the rude word is a humorous way to deflate what might become a tense situation.

7. **"No-asshole" rule:** The Foreign Exchange Institutional Sales team at ABN AMRO has instituted a no-asshole rule when it comes to hiring. Strong individual performance is not enough: Prospective employees need to fit into the culture.

8. **Tell the whole story:** Most companies try to put a positive spin on the stories they tell in formal communications, instead of reporting what actually occurred. Not every aspect of every project or initiative is executed perfectly, or turns out as planned. When you don't tell

the whole story, it's like you are deliberately trying to hide something. And, more importantly, no one can learn from other groups' successes or failures. Newsletters and other communication vehicles should address the same issues that people are whispering about in the hallways: what went wrong, how the participants tried to fix the problem, and what to do differently going forward. Telling the story the way it actually happened also shows people how collaboration really works, instead of the myth of how it works.

You too can encourage the flow of ideas in your workgroup by following these steps:

*1) Allow People to Vent*

When things happen that are out of their control, but which require changes to be made, people have an emotional reaction. It's very important to assemble the team members in a room and let them gripe. Allow them to say how they feel—to air their frustration—so they can get past their emotions and have room to think.

Many leaders fear letting people talk about their feelings because they believe it will create a negative atmosphere. While it's true that if people were to complain indefinitely, it would have a negative effect on the workgroup, remember that the negative feelings are already there. If they're not expressed verbally, they'll be expressed through behavior. People may have accidents, get sick, or try to sabotage the team. The trick is to set a time limit for the venting. Limit it to no more than an hour, depending on how serious the issue is.

The Midlands Development team at UNITE Group PLC found a way to address the emotional issues that go along with working in a stressful business with talented people who are highly invested in the success of their company. The UK-based company develops, owns, and manages affordable residences for students.

"When the team started out, most people were reluctant to discuss problems openly. . . . [A]s a team we went through a very black period where we had a number of projects going on at sites and . . . we suddenly all realized that we were just beating each other up all the time [instead of] dealing with problems properly," said former team leader Tim Mitchell. When they did discuss problems, people would take things personally—either by taking the blame themselves or assigning it elsewhere.

As a result, they decided to dial down the emotions and approach problems more positively. "We basically said . . . everybody's going to make mistakes from time to time, or a problem's going to arise, whether it's acquisition or design or planning . . . [and] we're just going to deal with them," Mitchell said. "We're not going to go over and try to dissect all the ins and outs, how we got where we are. We're just going to move forward and fix it. . . . Instead of it being your own problem, you've got eight or ten brains on it and everything can be solved in one way or another."

Mitchell compared the team to a shock absorber. "The shock absorber just bounces . . . and that's what it's designed to do. And [in] the development business, we should be designed to just absorb the shock and get on with it."

*2) Identify the Negative Assumptions and Then Reverse Them*
Negative assumptions get in the way of brainpower (see How Do You See It?). Whether the assumptions are true or not, they limit your ability to think through the possibilities. Put all the assumptions up on the board, and then systematically ask, "What if the opposite were true?"

I once worked with the leaders of a pharmaceutical company who had recently gotten some bad press that they felt wasn't warranted. They also believed that the company had done some noteworthy humanitarian work that was not covered in the media. Their assumption was that reporters wanted to see them as bad guys who were just out for the money and didn't care about people. I pointed out that as long as they accepted that assumption, there was nothing they could do to solve the problem. Therefore, they had nothing to lose by reversing the negative assumptions. The worst that would happen was that they would be unable to influence the reporters' perceptions.

When the group reversed the negative assumptions, the questions became, "What if the press respects our company? What if reporters think we do a lot of good work?" That approach opened up their thinking, and they were able to come up with numerous strategies to change the perception of the media.

## How Do You See It?

Negative assumptions get in the way of brainpower. They limit your ability to think through the possible ways to solve a problem. Here's how to reverse your negative assumptions.

| Negative assumption | Positive assumption |
| --- | --- |
| Inflexible | Principled |
| Risk-averse | Protective |
| Troublemaker | Courageous |
| Never satisfied | Sets high standards |
| Overly emotional, hyperbolic | Inspirational |
| Opinionated | Passionate |
| Rude | Straightforward |
| Indecisive | Flexible |

### 3) Generate Ideas

Let the ideas flow. Don't talk about what's wrong with the idea or why it won't work. That tends to "shut down" the person who suggested it. "The first response is going to be

American River College Library

to kill the idea or note the flaws," said creativity expert Blair Miller. You need to ask, "Is it more important to get rid of that idea as soon as possible, or is it more important that you deliberately promote an environment that facilitates high performance? If you get good at it, you can acknowledge ideas, not just murder them."

Research shows that true creativity happens after idea fourteen. However, most groups find it very difficult not to immediately eliminate ideas. That's because we're used to being rewarded for pointing out the negatives. But as I mentioned earlier, that simply fosters emotional responses and stifles brainpower. It's much more effective to encourage all ideas.

That's what Thaddeus Grimes-Gruczka, a supervisor at a large public relations agency, does. "One of my key goals as a supervisor has been to try to get people to come out of their shells. I say, 'Look, there are no bad ideas, there are only ideas you don't share. And if it's not a great idea no one's going to humiliate you, but you never know, you might have a gem,'" he said. The beauty is that even if the idea isn't brilliant, it may spawn a gem from someone else.

*4) Identify What's Smart About Each Idea, and Look for the Patterns That Emerge*

Although the typical brainstorming session quickly evolves into identifying what's wrong with ideas, you want to do the opposite and point out what's right. Go through each idea and look at what's smart about it. You'll see a pattern of recurring themes emerging. Make sure that all the themes are covered when you blend the ideas into a solution. By combining ideas, rather than eliminating them, the whole group takes ownership of the outcome.

*Collaboration Model*

High-performing workgroups get extraordinary results because the group owns the solutions to their problems. The following model delineates the steps.

- **Vent:** Assemble team members in a room and allow them to vent. Encourage them to say how they feel—to air their frustration—so they can get past their emotions and have room to think.
- **Reverse negative assumptions:** Identify the negative assumptions and then reverse them. Put all the assumptions up on the board, and then systematically ask, "What if the opposite were true?"
- **Generate ideas:** Let the ideas flow. Don't talk about what's wrong with the idea or why it won't work.
- **Identify what's smart:** Go through each idea and look at what's smart about it. You'll see a pattern of recurring themes emerging. Make sure that all the themes are covered when you blend the ideas into a solution. By

combining ideas, rather than eliminating them, the whole group takes ownership of the outcome.

· **Pinpoint the dangers:** The group needs to think about what could go wrong.

· **Develop an action plan:** You need to complete the preceding steps before you develop a plan.

*5) Identify the Dangers*

After the group has come up with the best idea or solution, it's time to look at the potential dangers ahead. Participants need to figure out what could go wrong. Because everyone owns the idea, group members are extraordinarily motivated to eliminate the obstacles. If the risks can't be overcome, they need to rethink the idea.

"When you authentically, with intellectual rigor, identify what's good about an idea, and then you look at what the possibilities are, the obstacles, hurdles that need to be overcome—it sends a clear message to the people bringing the ideas and to the organization that ideas are welcome here," noted Miller.

*6) Develop an Action Plan*

Most teams are good at developing a plan. However, if you don't complete the preceding steps first, chances are that the plan won't be robust enough to increase the workgroup's performance. Remember, our study found that creating a plan and measuring against goals is necessary but not sufficient: Both high-performing and nonperforming workgroups do these things. What distinguishes high-performing groups is that they create a learning environment such as the one described above.

People in high-performing groups feel strongly that the whole is greater than the sum of its parts. They work together, adopting an "all for one, one for all" mentality. When they make a decision, each person on the team has a stake. When everyone is involved, it "makes you feel like 'we're all part of this together and what we do is significant and important,'" said one study respondent who works at a major aerospace company.

## Pass the Ball

When using the collaboration model, it's important to take advantage of the different abilities that each person brings to the table. High-performing groups that I have observed play to the strengths of their members. They figure out who's good at what and they pass the ball to the right player. Members have informal roles, such as the person who is willing to get in there and get her hands dirty, or the diplomat who gets what the team needs from top management.

At one international chemical research and development firm, the executive team was comprised of the CEO and the heads of business development, marketing, finance, and operations. In addition to their functions, each person took a different perspective based on his own natural strengths.

For example, the CEO was the visionary—he had a talent for seeing opportunities. The head of operations was the opposite—he was always able to identify the risks. The business development person brought context and history to the discussion. The marketing person was attuned to how the workforce would react. Together, they made an effective team.

A workgroup in a logistics company makes sure that people with complementary strengths interact with clients. One member "has a way of walking into the room and being able to . . . turn a problem into an opportunity, smooth feathers, and make everybody feel good about what's going on," said the team's leader. Another member is the "secret weapon for getting out there on that shipping dock and making everyone feel 'yes, we've done the right thing by bringing the company in.' He's there, he's in front of them, he's getting the answers that they need." A third is the "fireman." When the inevitable glitches occur, he "is wonderful about sitting down with people and getting to the root cause of whatever the problem is, and he has a very good way about him also," the leader noted.

When Massachusetts-based Cookson Electronics wanted

to put together a team of top executives to reengineer the company's business process, it looked for people with different functional areas of expertise. "But we also needed people who had vision, who were able to change and adjust as you went along, to rethink," said Bill Affanato, who was a member of the group. Cookson, a capital equipment business that serves the electronics and semiconductor industry, was hit hard when the electronics market crashed in 2001.

"What made the team chemistry work was our attitudes towards work, our willingness to make it right no matter what the consequences . . . and kind of a personal thing where we all respected each other, which is a very large part of it," Affanato said. "It's really important to understand somebody else's opinion and trust their opinion to go forward."

If everyone on the team understands each other's particular strengths, it is much easier to trust their opinion. At GreenHouse Communications, a fifteen-year-old Chicago-based marketing communications agency, this became abundantly clear when the firm faced a difficult dilemma. "We have a culture and environment that says 'go, go, go, go, go' yet we had one of our most senior top-talented and accomplished individuals saying often 'slow, slow, slow.' We had a huge conflict brewing over this clash," explained Sandra House, chairman and CEO. The firm was in danger of losing the senior person, who was perceived as an obstructionist by others in the company.

At the same time, House wanted to expand the company's track record as an innovative and entrepreneurial shop. She brought in a consultant who administered an assessment to determine the thinking styles of the staff. The four thinking styles—ideator, clarifier, developer, and implementer—are all necessary for effective collaboration. It turned out that the firm had a preponderance of two thinking styles: ideator and implementer. The only developer—the one who takes a proposed solution and refines, improves, and evaluates whether it is workable—was the person on the verge of leaving.

"[The assessment] not only gives each individual an appreciation of where they find their natural energy in the problem-solving process, but it helps individuals . . . feel comfortable passing the ball when the group has to tackle part of the process that they're not so comfortable in," House said. "A light bulb went on, not only in this individual but in the group." The other members realized that they aren't comfortable with the developer role, "so we need to start listening to this developer more. When she's saying 'slow, slow, slow,' we should take her seriously, not think she's a roadblock. . . . That was hugely helpful to us."

As a result, the developer felt more empowered to raise difficulties she perceived in the agency's decision-making process. The group worked together to resolve several issues basic to the functioning of the firm. "We have great expectations for the new structure that emerged from this problem-solving session," House said. The agency added a discipline leader and created two new groups, promotions and design. Early results are very positive. In the first few months, the firm added two major new clients between the new groups, which were expected to account for at least 50 percent of the agency's growth in 2004.

In this chapter, I discussed ways high-performing workgroups can increase their performance. This is the fastest way to spread performance in your company. However, you don't want to ignore the rest of your organization.

Our study found that 52 percent of workgroups are average performing, what we call the "almost-there's." Let's assume that there is a similar distribution in your company. If you were able to move just 20 percent of the almost-there workgroups into the top category, you could catapult the company into a position to achieve sustainable growth. In Chapter 5, I'll show you how.

## Key Points

- The fastest, most effective way to achieve profitable growth is to focus on increasing the performance of your company's workgroups.
- The single most important quality necessary for leaders to foster a high-performing environment is honesty about themselves.
- To increase high performance, companies need to conduct 360-degree feedback on the environment of their workgroups.
- The two most important rules in respectful communication are: Always assume good intent; and identify the logic.
- People in high-performing groups feel strongly that the whole is greater than the sum of its parts. They work together, adopting an "all for one, one for all" mentality.
- High-performing groups play to the strengths of their members. They figure out who's good at what, and they pass the ball to the right player.

## Unexpected Findings

- Even your highest-performing business units have the capacity to do better. In the study, we asked survey participants to rate their workgroups from 0 to 10 on a series of performance measures. On average, those who belonged

to high-performing workgroups rated their group's performance at 7.0; they scored no measure higher than 7.8.
· We were not able to identify a "one size fits all" leadership style in high-performing groups. However, the environments that foster high performance are remarkably
similar around the world.

# CHAPTER 5

# Move the Middle

Your company has likely used some version of the collaboration model discussed in Chapter 4 to solve complex problems. You've gotten people together to brainstorm ideas, and if you followed the rules of respectful communication, you've probably reached a satisfactory solution—or maybe a brilliant one.

You may even have successfully stimulated your high-performing workgroups to do better work, or at least gotten out of their way so they can continue to excel. But to really accelerate high performance, you need to reach into your average-performing workgroups and help bring them to the next level. This chapter will show you how you can extend the collaboration model to "move the middle." By bringing your high-performing workgroups together with those that are "almost there," you can enhance the overall performance of your company.

If we assume that the performance distribution in your

own company is similar to the distribution in our global study of knowledge workers, 10 percent of your workgroups are high performing, 52 percent average performing, and 38 percent nonperforming. As you recall, we defined high-performing groups as those that made money for the company and created something new, such as a product or service. Average-performing groups were able to provide evidence of performance in profit, revenue, process improvement, product improvement, or one of five other business measures (see Appendix 1 for details). Nonperforming workgroups could not provide evidence of performance on any of those measures.

When most companies think about improving performance, they focus on the nonperforming workgroups. They eliminate the weakest business units and fire employees they perceive to be the least effective. Lopping off the bottom may reduce costs, but it does nothing to increase revenues. It may positively affect short-term profits; however, it won't help you develop new products, services, or markets. You can't cut your way to success.

On the other hand, transforming the whole company takes time and money that some companies don't have. If you're willing to put the necessary resources into a culture change initiative, it can lead to impressive results. However, transformations are large, complicated projects that require getting people to cooperate with you for a long time before they see lasting benefits. These efforts often involve expensive outside consultants. They may start off with a lot of energy, but at times when the going gets tough, they can lose momentum in favor of more manageable short-term projects.

There is another solution, which can be undertaken independently, or in conjunction with an ongoing transformation initiative. You can focus on transforming the workgroups that fall in the middle—those that already are getting some things right. As the chart illustrates, by moving fewer than 20 percent of the average-performing workgroups into the high-performing category, you can double the number of high-performing groups and substantially increase profitable growth. (See You Can Move the Middle.)

By moving the middle, you can get radical results—but the scope is more manageable than a transformation initiative, and the process can be scaled up as appropriate. The change agents are not outside consultants, but the

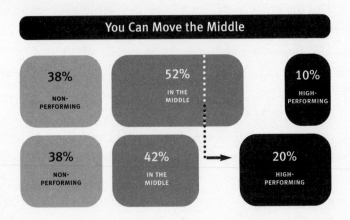

high-performing workgroups within your own company. These groups know where the obstacles and roadblocks to performance are, and they have the secrets for success.

I have observed many of these high-performing workgroups over the years. They all create an environment that values people, optimizes critical thinking, and seizes opportunities. In addition, three qualities set them apart (see Characteristics of High-Performing Groups).

First, they know how to quickly adapt to the changing external economic environment because they know their business and industry well, and they can capitalize on opportunities that arise. High-performing groups are often first movers with new products and services. They are usually ahead of the curve in recognizing a paradigm shift—in understanding how the world is changing and using that information to their company's advantage.

*Characteristics of High-Performing Groups*

High-performing workgroups:

- Quickly adapt to the changing economic environment
- Are customer-oriented, whether the customer is internal or external
- Know how to manage the internal corporate environment

Second, these groups are customer-oriented, whether the customer is internal or external. They know what the customer needs and wants, both intuitively and based on research, and they meet those needs.

The third quality, often overlooked, is that high-performing workgroups know how to manage the internal corporate environment. They get the support they need from senior managers, important company influencers, and other groups they work with. They understand when to push the envelope and when to hold back. They are capable of bending some rules when it's necessary to move forward. And they achieve extraordinary results.

High-performing groups are rarely asked to share their secrets with the rest of the company. However, I believe that if companies would solicit the help of their top groups, they would be eager to respond. While these groups want their own unit to achieve results, they understand that the main goal is the overall success of the company. It is important for companies to make this goal explicit, as does Tom Mendoza, president of Network Appliance, an enterprise network storage solutions company.

"I expect [employees] to really care what happens to the company," Mendoza said. "I want them to care about their contribution as a group, and I want them to care about their contribution as an individual. All three of those have to be equally important and they have to be really, really, really important."

One executive of a leading global energy corporation

pointed out that "there's a mentality here that says we want to be one company and we want to be a great company."

The attitude is similar at Cendian, which does chemical logistics outsourcing. Everyone there understands that when the company is implementing a big project under a tight deadline, they can be called upon to drop what they are doing and help out. This sensibility is built into the company's culture. "I think from day one we give evidence that you've got to enjoy that type of environment when you come on board with us . . . I think it's part of the whole introduction to Cendian," said Jim Soggs, vice president of Human Resources and Administration.

## Sharing Secrets

Some organizations have initiated systematic efforts to improve the performance of the company as a whole by spreading the secrets of high-performing workgroups. A common element of these initiatives is that they rely on internal—not external—resources.

The Bank of Ireland's Operations and Payments group, which is responsible for operations such as check clearance, cash distribution, and back-office processing, is recognized within the company and externally as high performing. In 2003, the group was named one of the "Best Companies to work for in Ireland" by the *Irish Independent* newspaper.

Operations and Payments also scored very well on a 2002 bank-wide survey conducted by the Gallup organization on employees' level of engagement. The Bank of Ireland results as a whole were "disappointing," according to Padraig Langan, HR manager for Operations and Payments, "however, our own results [were] absolutely through the roof." The Operations and Payments group scored 4.2 out of 5, compared to the bank's score of 3.5. In the seven units of the bank's Retail Division, the percentage of actively engaged employees ranged between 20 and 30; 62 percent of Operations and Payments employees were actively engaged. In addition, surveys conducted by the bank showed a customer satisfaction rating of about 80 percent for the group. "You looked at the other units and they were coming out somewhere between 40 to the mid-50s," Langan said.

A deliberate effort led to the high scores for Operations and Payments. Before 1995, operations work was decentralized in the branches. Although the work was critical, it was monotonous, and the people who did it felt undervalued. The bank decided to centralize the function into one unit, and "by doing that, giving it a sense of identity in itself; giving it a huge sense of value," said Langan. By focusing on customer service, efficiency, and valuing people, Operations and Payments became one of the highest-performing units in the organization.

In an effort to spread this success, bank management

decided to bring other workgroups under the wing of Operations and Payments. "There's now a broader view of what operations work is," Langan explained. The bank recently split Credit Cards and Loans, one of the larger units of the Retail Division, in two and moved the bigger chunk of employees under Operations and Payments. At the same time, the group permanently reassigned some of its best people to work with Credit Cards and Loans.

Rather than bringing in outside consultants to improve the performance of the Credit Cards group, the bank chose to use its own resources to accomplish that goal. "You now have to keep an eye on what is good—and don't let go of what is good—and in turn, bring up what is quite low," said Langan.

Langan acknowledged that the process is a huge challenge. "The journey of actually building up trust is a difficult one," he pointed out. Nevertheless, Langan expects this process to continue. "There are other chunks of operations that are going to come in under us," he said. The plan is for all the groups to reach the performance level of the best, thus improving the organization as a whole.

At Macquarie Capital Partners, a niche real estate investment bank, all employees get updates on current transactions and share ideas during an hour-long phone call every two weeks. The thirty-five-person firm, which was founded in January 2001, had a record year in fiscal 2003 in terms of revenue and transactions completed. It generated more than $2 million in revenue per principal, compared to an industry standard of $1 to $2 million, according to Managing Principal Don Suter.

"Everybody is engaged in that conversation because everyone benefits if that transaction is successful," according to Suter, who noted that ownership is pushed way down into the firm—much more so than at a Wall Street investment bank. For example, someone will introduce a potential transaction in which a client from the Middle East wants to invest in the high-end apartment market in central London. "There will be three or four people who will say 'we worked on a deal like that two years ago and you ought to talk to so-and-so,' " said Suter.

The biweekly conversation is "something that in my view you can do with a company that's our size but you can't do it if you have 4,500 employees," Suter noted.

You may not be able to do it exactly that way—but even very large companies can find ways to share information so that the secrets of high performers are spread throughout the organization. McDonald's, a company with 31,000 restaurants in 118 countries, has internal groups that specialize in every major aspect of its business—including food, equipment and operations, marketing, construction, and real estate—and work with franchisees globally to improve their performance.

"McDonald's is very good at nurturing operations around the world. They invest heavily in support structure—resources such as mine that come in and help improve the local and regional business in subject areas such as operations and equipment," said Bill Hallett, vice president of Worldwide Operations. Worldwide Operations provides consulting support to counterparts in other countries; other responsibilities include creating and protecting operating standards for the company.

"We may see France doing something that is very productive and is positively impacting sales and customer service. We would share that with Taiwan, who has a similar initiative and maybe has some challenges in that area," said Hallett.

McDonald's formed Worldwide Operations and Equipment in 1991 when senior management decided to consolidate the U.S. groups that worked part-time on international expansion into a separate division focused on international growth. Hallett's group was selected from among people who had line experience in equipment and operations, as well as expertise in international expansion.

Worldwide Operations has been particularly successful in increasing performance because of the collaborative, respectful approach it takes while working in other countries. "Although [the teams that do similar work] all get high marks, we get very high marks in terms of support," said Hallett. "Almost half my team is from outside the U.S. We are more diverse in terms of ethnicity, religion, and gender than most other groups in the corporate office."

Worldwide Operations tends to focus on the largest markets, but it works with countries that are in a variety of different situations. "We will go into a country doing really well to learn what they're doing so we can share that with other countries," said Hallett. The group also will work with countries that are on the verge of performing well, as well as with troubled countries facing customer service, sales, or execution challenges.

The latter was the case in Puerto Rico, where McDonald's has operated since the late 1960s. The business struggled in the late 1990s. "It was an underperforming market financially; underperforming in terms of customer satisfaction. It was an organization that didn't have a clear direction on where it wanted to go as a market," said Hallett. Nevertheless, Puerto Rico was committed to improve and had taken steps to identify the problems when the Worldwide Operations group agreed to work with them.

"We knew a number of the players in Puerto Rico well, and so we capitalized on the relationship. . . . [We] had a good working relationship on a variety of other projects, so we were able to hit the ground running together," Hallett noted. "What we did was have our experts come down and work with them to place renewed emphasis on training, renewed emphasis on operational execution across the front counter and through the drive-through. And we worked with them to implement a new production system . . . it was an integrated team."

The two groups collaborated throughout 2001 and 2002, and the results were impressive. Customer satisfaction scores increased by high single digits. Sales increased about 10 to 15 percent. Crew and licensee satisfaction scores increased from single figures to double digits and turnover went down by double digits. "Our team played a very strong role and I think we helped Puerto Rico to get over the hump," said Hallett. He takes pains not to take too much credit, however. "Puerto Rico took the lead in a side-by-side partnership over two years."

One global energy company took a different approach to sharing information. It recently brought all its partner-operated businesses, which had been intermingled with company-operated businesses, into a single performance unit. The heads of two of the partner-operated businesses started talking about common issues. "We were learning so much from each other that we said, 'let's get the rest of the gang together and start talking on a regular basis, and figure out how we can actually learn together and do something really powerful together,'" said Frank, one of the two leaders.

In addition to sharing information, the partner-operated businesses faced the common problem that their workgroups had been downsized significantly. "We're working to change the mentality of these teams that have all been cut and are questioning what their value is to understanding that these teams are fantastic places to be," Frank said. The people who fill the limited number of these slots have the opportunity to be intimately involved in every aspect of the business. "The only way I'm going to drive my team to fantastic performance is to give them a new identity. And the only way to give them a new identify is to create it within the segment." That necessitated working together.

With the blessing of the company, leaders from partner-operated businesses throughout the world met together for a three-day session. "It was really powerful to get together and share experiences and understand we all have the same stresses and concerns," Frank said.

Among the outcomes of the session was a "complexity index" that allowed the group to compare the cost of very different businesses on an "apples to apples" basis. "All of a sudden you're no longer bashing the team with high costs, saying 'you're inefficient, your costs are all out of whack.' Now you can have a conversation that makes sense. We brought some of the best and brightest together to think this through and in general they agree that this index is a pretty fair indication of the complexity of this business."

## Move the Middle Model

Bank of Ireland, McDonald's, Macquarie, the energy company—each uses a different process, but the concept is the same: You can improve overall performance by spreading the secrets that are hidden in your own company. Based on my research and experience, I have created an intervention model for doing this that I believe offers the strongest possibility for success. It is based on bringing together a high-performing and an almost-there workgroup to create a SWAT team, whose goal is to improve the performance of both workgroups. As I explained in Chapter 4, high-performing groups have room to grow. Almost-there's have demonstrated the ability to make money for the company or to do something new but have not reached their full potential.

Under this model, both groups' performance is enhanced by the intellectual stimulation of collaborating and the common goal of benefiting the company. Both have a vested interest in the performance of their own group, which provides an incentive to succeed. Unlike the relationship between a consultant—whether internal or external—and a workgroup, both are in the trenches and face similar obstacles. If they identify a common problem that is inhibiting performance, their influence is now increased; the company is more motivated to address problems that affect multiple groups.

For this model to be effective, the initiative has to be driven by the company, which should assign an advocate such as a senior leader, business unit leader, or member of the executive team for each SWAT team. The advocate's job is to make sure the team understands that the goal of the effort is to increase company performance. She also has to make sure that the team gets the information and support it needs from the company.

Below is a step-by-step approach to moving the middle (see How to Move the Middle). I suggest that you start small, piloting the approach with a few teams. Then pair up more workgroups as you begin to see success.

- Identify the high- and average-performing workgroups in your company. Criteria that you can use to identify these groups are discussed in Chapter 4. (See Results the Right Way: The Environment of High-Performing Workgroups, page 74.)
- From the average-performing groups, choose the top 20 percent. Select these groups based on: accepted metrics such as unit profitability, EBITDA, ROI, etc.; how important the results are to the company; and

*How to Move the Middle*

1. Identify the high-performing and average-performing workgroups in your company.
2. Choose the top 20 percent of the average-performing groups—the almost-there's.
3. Create SWAT teams made up of representatives of high-performing and almost-there groups. Assign a member of the senior management team as an advocate for the SWAT team.
4. Set aside time on a regular basis for the SWAT teams to meet.
5. Tell the real story of the SWAT team as it is unfolding.

whether the groups value people, optimize critical thinking, and seize opportunities. Choose the groups that can make the biggest difference in the least amount of time.

- Match an almost-there group with a high-performing group. Link groups based on common functions, goals, or clients. Groups that have worked together in the past and already have established a good relationship are ideal.

- Create a SWAT team made up of representatives of both groups. Representatives should be selected by the leader of each group and their direct reports. Choose a total of eight to ten people who have a demonstrated track record of overcoming obstacles and who have earned credibility and respect among coworkers. Make sure that you select individuals with complementary functional expertise and natural strengths, as discussed in Chapter 3. Assign a member of the senior management team as an advocate for the SWAT team.

  Set aside time on a regular basis for representatives of the high-performing and the almost-there groups to work together as a team. The SWAT team should set goals and identify problems that the two groups have in common, as well as those that are unique to each. The team should jointly address the problems. Members of both groups should share what's worked for them. By collaborating, both the high-performing and the almost-there workgroups benefit.

My experience is that smart people who are not embroiled in the day-to-day functioning of a group often can see things in a different way. In fact, when I bring a problem that a client is experiencing to my graduate students at the University of Chicago, they frequently come up with alternative solutions because they see the situation from a fresh perspective. Other people from the company may be brought in to consult with the SWAT team as needed. The team should continue meeting until the goals are achieved and reconvene quarterly to make sure the results are sustained.

· Tell the story of the teams throughout the company as it is unfolding through both formal and informal channels. Make SWAT team members responsible for sharing their experiences. Hold meetings to discuss the collaboration, and allow people to ask questions and make suggestions about how it might work better. Share both successes and failures of the SWAT team as part of the learning process.

While companies often give lip service to the idea of learning from their mistakes, many are never willing to talk about them. Telling the story is critical because it shows how collaboration really works, instead of the myth of how it works. The more honest you are about what actually occurred, the more likely you are to get dramatic results. "The organization [can] actually learn more from the bad experiences than from

the good experiences sometimes," said Håkan Bryn-
gelson, CEO of Vasakronan, the largest commercial
real estate company in Sweden. "We discuss [mis-
takes] in open groups or we actually go out and talk
about it in a wider sense," he added. Vasakronan was
one of the best companies to work for in Sweden in
2003, according to Oxford Research AB.

Many companies hope to increase performance by improving operations, learning more about their customers, and trying to do more with less. While these
strategies may increase a company's profit margin, they
do not lead to profitable growth. To grow, companies
must learn what their high-performing workgroups are
doing right and spread that knowledge. Organizations
such as McDonald's, Macquarie Capital, Bank of Ireland,
and others have successfully shared the secrets of high
performers. I believe that it's worth a shot. You have
nothing to lose.

## Countering Resistance

The biggest obstacle to success in a move-the-middle process is the natural tendency for people to keep their secrets
to themselves. However, as I mentioned earlier, high-
performing workgroups tend to understand that the company's performance is more important than that of a

workgroup or an individual. Top leaders must deliberately encourage the sharing of ideas.

That's what Pierre de Villemejane did when he was the president of Cookson Electronics. Although the company, a capital equipment manufacturer, had created a cross-functional team of top executives to reengineer its business processes before de Villemejane became division president, he was the group's key proponent. "I think they needed some executive support. That was their main concern," he said.

One way he supported the team, called TOPS (technology, operations, people, and strategy), was by acting as a mediator when it encountered resistance to change. De Villemejane continually explained to business unit leaders the project's importance to the company's future health and strategic advantage, and "made it clear to the organization that there was no room for negotiation" in the way the project was implemented.

"Obviously that helped," de Villemejane said. "There was no way I was going to spend eighteen months and the expense we had spent only to . . . have different sets of processes and different systems being implemented in two sites."

Bill Affanato, a member of the TOPS team, said at the time, "He's our number one fan. He's our arbitrator when we have discussions with other vice presidents and we're trying to implement changes that people are a little sketchy or nervous about," he said. "He went out and championed us in a lot of ways."

By personally embracing the project and staying on top of the details, de Villemejane signaled its importance to the entire company. He made sure that the executive team and all employees were regularly updated on the team's progress "to keep people enthused on a project that is eighteen months long, where you don't see a lot of benefit until you flip the switch."

Sheryl Chin, senior manager of the Client Implementation team at Cendian, also emphasized the role of company leadership in heading off potential resistance to collaboration. "Our president has walked around and talked to people. He has expressed how important [implementation] is, so I have people literally saying 'what can I do to help on this project?' on a daily basis," she said.

"I don't have to go knocking on doors to get resources. Resources are knocking on our door. . . . We have vice presidents who come to us and say 'how can my organization help you further?' We have analysts who come and say 'how can we help you further?' It's throughout the organization, a total alignment toward the objectives."

Bill Hallett's Worldwide Operations group at McDonald's overcomes resistance by establishing good personal relationships with colleagues in other countries. According to Kamran Shaukat, a member of the group, "Under Bill's leadership the main thing is the human contact: I mean this is a big company, 30,000 restaurants plus. But the folks here would know their equipment manager, say in China, intimately. They would know he has a wife, how many children, and their names."

Hallett is careful about who is on his team. Members have to recognize "that Pakistan or Brazil or Germany is not the U.S. I tend to hand pick people. . . . There are some folks who just are not cut out to deal with other cultures. They don't like the food, they don't like the travel, they don't like the language differences," Hallett said.

Team members try not to dictate solutions. According to Shaukat, "It is rare for our department to come and say 'this is a mandate: redo it.' It's always left up to [the country]. We give them all the tools, the guidance, the help, we go down there. But the final decision will be theirs."

All of the high-performing workgroups I've come across emphasize that respect for colleagues' skills and talents is critical. Without this respect, high-performing groups risk becoming used-to-be's. The Hudson Highland Center for High Performance study found that 38 percent of workgroups were nonperforming. Of those nonperforming workgroups, 29 percent used to perform at a higher level than they do today. Something happened to get in the way of high performance. In Chapter 6, I'll look at what went wrong and explain how you can avoid making the same mistakes.

## Key Points

- By bringing high-performing workgroups together with those that are almost there, you can enhance the overall performance of your company.
- When most companies think about improving performance, they focus on eliminating the nonperforming workgroups and firing the least effective employees. However, you can't cut your way to success.
- Focus on transforming the workgroups that fall in the middle—those that already are getting some things right.
- Use internal change agents to move the middle.
- The biggest obstacle in a move-the-middle process is the natural tendency for people to keep their secrets to themselves. Top leaders must deliberately encourage the sharing of ideas.

# CHAPTER 6

# How to Destroy High Performance

"[Our workgroup is] wonderfully demoralized. With the restructuring, I figure there's probably a handful of people who actually want to go in to work at this point, and everybody else wishes they had gotten the severance package," said a senior scientist at a leading food and beverage company.

"I have never seen a company that functions this beautifully with so much of a mental handicap. Have you ever met a person who at home is abusive or violent or insane . . . but that person shows up at work every day like clockwork and does a great job? This is the sort of thing I'm seeing here. You peel back the outer layers of this real classy looking organization and you see putrescence and gangrene," said an associate director of sourcing at a large pharmaceutical company.

"We have a meeting once a month to go over our results," said a controller at a commercial printing company.

"[For] our production numbers, we're meeting our target in almost every single category we have for the year. But I would be willing to bet that there will be something that we'll get challenged on that's not good enough."

Given the level of frustration that these knowledge workers express about their work environment, it is highly unlikely that they can do their best thinking—the thinking that leads to profitable growth for the company.

Tom Mendoza, now president of Network Appliance, told me about the time he was sitting with the CEO of a for-mer company when a line manager walked in to the office. "I could tell he was so pumped because he and this other person had done so much work. The CEO read the first page and a half, ripped it in half and said 'I do not agree with these ideas.' And I said [to the CEO], 'You know, you might want to just post your ideas on the door and just save everybody a lot of time. . . . You hire smart people and then you've got to encourage them to think. What do you think you just did with that?' "

During my two decades as a business consultant and professor, I have heard many stories from a broad range of companies and industries about how organizations inhibit high performance. Employees at large and small corpora-tions, industrial and service companies, blue chips and entrepreneurial start-ups—all have stories to tell about behaviors that extinguish thinking.

Although these negative behaviors run the gamut from lack of appreciation to sexual harassment, the ones most frequently mentioned in our study are micromanaging, hoarding information, and leaders acting in their own self-interest. In some cases, people are simply not good managers—they don't have the right skills to foster environments in which employees can do their best work. A much larger problem, however, is the effect of short-term focus on performance.

As a result of market forces such as globalization and commoditization, companies feel they must focus on the short term. Public companies face the added pressure of keeping shareholders happy. As Shell UK Chairman Clive Mather put it when I asked him about challenges facing his company, "We are required—all major corporations are—to jump through hoops every quarter."

A survey conducted in late 2003 by professors at the Duke University Fuqua School of Business and the University of Washington indicates the problem is widespread. The survey involved financial executives at 401 companies and included in-depth interviews with a score of senior executives.

When asked how they would respond to a situation in which earnings could potentially come in under target, nearly 80 percent said they would decrease discretionary spending on things such as research, advertising, and maintenance in an effort to meet the target. If an opportunity arose that would boost long-term profitability but, in all probability, bring down short-term earnings, 41 percent said they would not pursue the project if it meant missing the quarterly target.

In an interview with the *Wall Street Journal,* one of the researchers confessed surprise that financial officers were eager to talk about foregoing long-term gain to put a better spin on short-term earnings.

While reducing expenses, cutting staff, and living quarter to quarter may drive short-term profitability, it is killing high performance. The Hudson Highland Center for High Performance study found that nearly 40 percent of respondents could offer no evidence that their workgroups were doing something tangible to contribute to the company's performance. These workgroups, comprised of well-educated, well-paid people, are not coming up with new products, services, or markets—nor are they making money for the company.

Equally troubling is that almost one-third of the respondents in nonperforming workgroups classified their groups as used-to-be's. They once were high performing, but no longer are.

The research found that members of both high-performing and nonperforming groups feel overworked and at the mercy of short-term goals. Asked to rate how closely certain statements apply to their workgroups, study respondents gave the lowest scores to the following (a low score means that the statement does not apply to the respondent's workgroup):

- The group promotes work/life balance
- Personal needs are taken into account
- Long-term success outweighs short-term goals

The gap in scores between high-performing and non-performing workgroups was also the smallest for these statements, meaning these factors inhibit the performance of both types of groups. As you will recall from Chapter 4, even high-performing groups have room to grow.

Knowledge workers are working too hard; they are putting in too many hours and sacrificing their personal lives. Their companies are focused on short-term financial goals. All of this gets in the way of performance. It's understandable that companies are cutting costs to increase profits. However, the study indicates that the way they are cutting—and how deep they are cutting—is affecting their ability to grow profitably. Profitable growth requires companies to differentiate themselves through new products and services. But they are inadvertently killing the environment that allows these innovations to thrive.

Short-term thinking ultimately turned Hal Thompson's high-performing workgroup into a used-to-be. Thompson (not his real name) was in charge of an ad agency workgroup that was the best performing of four divisions. The group had nearly tripled its gross revenues in ten years. During that period it had gone from minimal profitability to a 10 to 13 percent profit margin. "We [the workgroup] had taken on a loss operation and cre-

*Behaviors That Prevent/Destroy High Performance*

*Show Disrespect*
- Do the thinking for smart people
- Embarrass with public criticism
- Humiliate people when they fail

*Hoard Information*
- Control who receives information
- Protect from bad news
- Guard best practices as proprietary secrets

*Micromanage*
- Limit responsibilities
- Dictate every expected outcome
- Tell how you want something done

*Shirk Responsibility*
- Assume others will do what's necessary
- Wait to be asked
- Blame others for mistakes

*Pursue Personal Agenda*
- Seek personal gains
- Focus on your own success
- Never share credit

*Undervalue Learning*
- Eliminate training
- Hide what you learn

ated a profitable, growing, well-respected company," he said.

"We had good clients. We did good work, and it appeared from the outside, and this was true, that the company cared about the employees." The agency was flexible in terms of the workplace and work hours. It compensated people fairly. People had opportunities to attend industry meetings. "People felt like they could develop their career," Thompson said.

Then the company was acquired by a large global agency. When the new parent company came in, it set strict margin and profit requirements. "There just was simply no way to get there short of cutting in the short term," he explained. "We looked at everything we could possibly cut other than people." The summer outing and the Christmas party were eliminated. The rented plants were history. The management instituted a hiring freeze, cut back on travel, and stopped sending people to seminars and industry meetings. They stopped giving raises.

Junior people began to quit because they felt they would have more opportunities elsewhere. Clients questioned why people were leaving, and some abandoned the agency. Thompson eventually was forced to lay off people.

Thompson did not accept all this quietly. He went to the people in charge and warned that the division was losing people and hemorrhaging clients. "The response was, 'Well, since you're losing clients, you're going to have to cut even further,'" Thompson said.

Thompson tried to support staff members who were working with clients, shielding them from the budget conversations and the pressure to cut. "I kept as much of it from them as I could because it would just make morale that much worse and make them much more desperate and frustrated." At the same time, he advocated for his group with top management, presenting formal one-, two-, and three-year plans to get the division back on track. He asked for margin relief in the short term to enable gross revenues to increase. "[The plans] were just ignored, you know, just completely dismissed," Thompson said.

"The most absurd part of it was that through these series of cuts and adjustments, both personnel and nonpersonnel stuff, we got our margin quite a bit higher, but the actual number of dollars, the profit dollars we were giving them declined by 30 percent."

It took Thompson a year before he realized that the situation was not going to improve. "I wanted to believe that I could get these people to come around and see what we've done here, what we're capable of doing and how we've done it, and then they'll, of course, be more than willing to support us." But it didn't happen and he began looking for another job.

When he submitted his resignation after fourteen years, the company quickly agreed to his terms. "I was just not a good boy. I didn't do things the way they wanted." Before he left, he put together a plan to keep the unit going. About eight people left at the same time, with severance Thompson negotiated. He had seen the number of employees dwindle from eighty to thirty-two. He watched profits shrink and clients depart. A high-performing group was decimated, on its way to extinction.

It didn't have to be that way. Although clearly the company needed to meet financial goals, senior managers could have worked with Thompson to figure out how to do so without losing the environment that fostered high performance. The company failed to take advantage of the intellectual assets it acquired when it bought the firm.

Unfortunately, Thompson's is not the only company that interfered with a good thing and destroyed it. Frank Benton's experience is another example of how high performance can be achieved and how easily it can be destroyed. Benton (not his real name) works in research and development for a software company. Assigned the task of dramatically upgrading an existing software program, Benton assembled a team of IT developers and infused them with an intense sense of ownership in the project.

Upper management initially gave Benton's team twelve months to complete the task, but soon reduced the deadline to seven months to accelerate the project's profitability. Still, the team completed the work on time with excellent results. Company executives then concluded that the work could be done with fewer developers, so two members of Benton's team were laid off.

In the next round of development, Benton again was

able to motivate his team members, and again they not only met the deadline but beat it. Subsequently, two more team members were laid off. "The people who worked for me did such a fine job. We were on time, on schedule, and made money. We hit all of our sales quotas, but yet I lost team members. . . . It bugged me because here we did such a fine job but yet we got hammered for it," Benton said. "We finally lost the whole team. . . . The company just sees it as an upside because they get more profits."

Even if Benton's company made a legitimate decision to eliminate a line of business to maximize profits, it failed to recognize that more was at stake than a few jobs. Had Benton been a partner in the decision-making process, he might have helped find a way for the group to continue to improve products and stimulate profitable growth for the company. By decimating a high-performing team and demoralizing the leader, the company unintentionally undermined the kind of innovation it needs to succeed in the long term.

Frank Benton believes he was punished for success. Unfortunately, this phenomenon is more common than you might think. An assistant vice president in the finance department at a leading global financial services firm said that's what happened to his high-performing team. When people were let go "to weed out the dead weight," his group took on additional responsibilities. "It seems to be obvious that they were trying to force people to do more for less," he said.

"I think because we were able to take on the additional

responsibilities, they [thought], 'Hey, even though they were overworked, they got the job done, and maybe in the future we can just have them continue to do it. We don't have to hire anybody. . . . ' Being efficient and effective actually hurt us in the sense that we have additional responsibilities now but there's no reward for it. So, sometimes being really good at what you do is not necessarily a good thing."

Companies may save money by cutting staff, but they lose a great deal more by demoralizing high performers and taking away the resources they need to do their best work. Our study found that many of the behaviors that stifle high performance are the opposite of those you need to achieve high performance—valuing people, optimizing thinking, and seizing opportunities. Seventy-one percent of those who believe their companies stifle high performance said they did so by "not enough funding," "not enough people," "no career path," and "not enough training" (see Appendix 4 for an explanation of how this number was derived).

The same percentage mentioned behaviors such as "threatening, dishonest," "only concerned with profit, bottom line," "centralized control," and "unsupportive" as stifling high performance.

## There's Another Way

Some companies are seeking ways to meet short-term goals without sacrificing high performance in the long term.

Macquarie Capital Partners, for example, has decided to focus on the big picture. "We're running a marathon and we're in the first mile," said Don Suter, managing principal of the boutique investment bank. "If we're going to do something that hasn't been done before, this group has to stay together, they have to stay energized, this has to be the place that they want to work forever."

As a result of this attitude, Suter spends a lot of time urging employees to spend more time with their wives and children. He tells them, "If you find a situation where you can get out of the office one evening early and go home and spend some time with your family, that's not frowned upon, that's encouraged." He added, "We do about everything we can to discourage people from working here on the weekends."

Suter contrasts this environment with that of other investment banks. "[In Wall Street firms], the deal that's been made between the husband/father and the rest of the family is, 'I am going to go away for ten years and I am going to make more money than you can ever imagine. And the price for that is I'm not going to see you very much. But once we have more money than we can ever imagine I'm going to retire and do something else.' That is the Wall Street mentality, but it's not ours," Suter said.

Brown Brothers Harriman, a New York-based investment services firm, also stays focused on the long term. According to Andrew Tucker, a partner in the firm and chairman of its European subsidiaries, in a downturn, "[people] think that the sky is falling. Therefore, [they] take severe measures to reduce expenditures and headcount, stop doing forward-thinking projects, and just focus on daily survival." He added that after a period of having fewer people do more and more, "eventually you reach a point where that is no longer tenable." He acknowledged that "you have to take steps to adjust to the current economic environment," but with a clear line of sight to the future.

For example, Tucker pointed to a large competitor that eliminated 10 percent of its workforce during a downturn. "By the time they actually achieve the savings from that draconian measure, which typically is about eighteen months, the economy has turned and they're starting to hire again. In the meantime, they have the cost of rehiring and the morale cost of the survivors wondering if they are going to be next," Tucker said. Instead of large-scale layoffs, Brown Brothers Harriman took the long-term view, sharpening its performance measures to make firing decisions on an individual basis.

"Your best assets go up and down in the elevator every day. . . . You have got to pay a lot of attention to that in good times and bad," Tucker said.

## Destructive Behaviors

Many of the people interviewed for our study work in environments in which they are not trusted and are not encouraged to think. Their leaders undermine their own potential for success by micromanaging, hoarding information, and putting personal interests first. These self-defeating practices are a throwback to an earlier form of management common in the industrial economy. They also are human responses to vulnerability and uncertainty. However, in today's economy, when knowledge workers must come up with innovations that will make money for the company, these destructive behaviors have more significant consequences than in the past.

Micromanaging is the most efficient way to block high performance since it negates all three factors necessary for a high-performance environment. When a leader micromanages, he demonstrates that he doesn't respect his group members, stifles original thinking, and discourages the group from seizing opportunities.

As one survey respondent put it, "You're given a task to do [yet] . . . they don't seem to trust you to get it done, so you have somebody on your back every day asking, 'Have you got it done yet?' And the only reason they're on your back is because their boss is on their back."

This kind of behavior has the opposite effect of what was intended. "The people that are being micromanaged, they just get angry, get negative about the company and negative about their work."

Many people in the study voiced similar concerns. "[The leader who inhibited my performance] didn't seem to trust what I did," said Mike Anderson of a global pharmaceutical company. "He wanted to double check. He'd say, 'OK, go this far and then check back with me.' Well, that's a time waster because if I can't reach that guy right then, what do I do? . . . You can't move forward."

Another study participant who works for an aircraft company also felt stymied by micromanagement. "They've got to be involved in every little decision, every little thing that's done, and it does impede progress. . . . [You] get the feeling like gee, I can't go out on a limb or I can't go ahead and make decisions without running it up through the mill first, and it sort of dampens the enthusiasm."

Rather than fostering high performance, this approach stifles it. "The best way to get the worst work out of me is to stand over my shoulder, or question me," said survey respondent Thaddeus Grimes-Gruczka. "Give me a task, give me a deadline, and let's meet on this date and I'll show you where we are. Don't come into my office every day and say 'how's that going, what's up today, any news?' That is the worst way to manage me, and I think generally people don't like that. You know, you've hired me, you've given me responsibility, trust me. And if I'm horrible, fire me!"

He added, "Rather than just saying, 'Here's what I need you to do,' it's hammering you over the head with, 'Do you understand what I want? You're going to do this; you're going to do that,' and going over each step. And then when you bring it back to them, [it's] 'Why don't you do this?'

or, 'Why don't you do that?' So, you don't feel like you have the freedom to do what you need to do."

In one consumer products company, new management decided that every employee should develop three goals every sixty days. The problem was, according to a survey respondent, "our senior manager is such a micromanager it was difficult to get anything by him. He would change single words that he didn't like. . . . It took longer to write the goals than to get them done! That's a little bit of a stretch, but people were spending literally a week on three simple goals . . . to get them past senior management."

Workgroups can't do their best thinking under these conditions. "There's a certain amount of stifling of originality when you tell people how to do things. They are not using their minds. . . . [It] affects everything from how to promote a product for the first time, how to write systems, to even how to interact with each other," noted one respondent.

Leaders who trust their group members to get the job done engender much greater commitment than those who dictate every move. A study respondent who works for a consulting firm said that her boss is very hands off. "He says, 'Here's a project, go do it' and he doesn't check in with me every day to see if it's going OK. He doesn't follow up with other team members to see that they're getting what they need. He just assumes that I'm going to do it. . . . That's his style and I really like that. Every project that we've done has been that way. . . . I think it really forces me to be my best."

At Barrister Executive Suites, Inc., top management doesn't get in the way of people who are doing their jobs. "They have a lot of freedom if they perform well, and they're running their own show. If they're doing well and their billing is going up every month, nobody says anything to them except 'congratulations, you're doing a great job.' Nobody is calling them to say 'we need to do this and what about this and what about that.' You don't disturb them if they're doing great," said Vince Otte, chairman and CEO.

Many companies don't understand that, however. After enough micromanaging, people get fed up and leave. Scott Galloway, who was interviewed for the study, said he once worked for a manager who "didn't give you a lot of free rein, you didn't have the ability to . . . individualize the process to how it worked best for you. Ultimately that's what caused me to leave that company."

Another respondent told us about a new leader at the top "who has very specific beliefs on how things should be done." He said that the company's approach changed from one in which the company and the employee worked to-gether to figure out the best way to do things, to "you have to do it my way." As a result, he said, "We lost a lot of good people. And secondly, there is a huge morale hit because people are made to fit the mold that the business requires, and I think for at least half the people that I work with, that's a problem."

## Self-Interest

Group members who perceive that a leader has his or her own interest in mind—rather than the interests of the group and the company—are not going to do their best work.

"You've got to believe that when I ask you to do something . . . you never have a single moment where you say 'I wonder what's in it for him,'" said Tom Mendoza, of Network Appliance, one of *Fortune* magazine's "100 Best Companies to Work For" in 2004. He added, "If I say to you 'I really need you to do this,' it should be an honor to you because you know that I care a lot about [the issue], and I'm coming to you."

Unfortunately, many survey respondents said that they do question their leader's motives. A public relations executive talked about an important piece of business, worth several million dollars, that his firm lost after seven years. "The fact is people panicked," he said. "The person who had built that business over many years, who is very talented, began to try to play it politically at the company." Apparently worried about her future, she started trying to figure out who she needed to have lunch with.

"She was basically trying to play 'Politburo.' Remember in the old days of the Soviet Union when they had the big parades? They'd look up at the stand and see who was standing where, how close they were to the Soviet leader, and that's how they figured out what was going on? Well, that's what she was trying to do. And that's not what was needed. . . . [T]he way to solve it was to come up with some fresh ideas and a new team."

A marketing manager at an information collection and delivery company said her manager protects herself by refusing to take responsibility if there is a problem. "If something goes bad, then [my manager] is the first to pass it off as being somebody else's fault regardless of what the situation may have actually been," said the study respondent. In one situation, the manager approved a subordinate's work, but when the client complained about it, she blamed the subordinate and put him on a "performance plan." "He's quitting tomorrow. . . . The impact on morale is awful."

The opposite also happens: Leaders take credit for the accomplishments of people who work for them. One survey respondent pointed out that if people were working in a culture "where you knew good ideas were being stolen and others higher on the chart were taking credit for them . . . if you're a normal human being you would just shut down [and] go into a mode of 'I'm just going to do what I'm told, and that's it.' "

Tom Ross, an engineer who participated in the study, described a senior manager "who certainly was very much self-serving. He was interested in isolating senior managers from those of us who worked in development to make sure that he could take credit for whatever work that we did." Ross said another senior team leader "was interested in isolating herself more and more from the rest of us and excluding us from upper level meetings where our input certainly could have been useful." Ross ended up leaving the company because of the lack of communication.

At Ross's former company, upper-level managers were deprived of valuable input from developers. But equally important, the developers were deprived of information they needed to succeed. Although some leaders try to protect their own interests and enhance their power by hoarding information, it is ultimately self-defeating, since access to information is critical for knowledge workers to make money for the company.

Study respondent Teri Wysocky, who works in research and development, also felt she needed more information. "I couldn't do what I needed to do because I had no idea what upper management had already committed to. It was just a real lack of communication, [there was] no way to really figure out what it was that I should be doing and what I should be communicating to the team from R&D's side," she said.

A benefits consultant for pension plans said that information he needs seems to be deliberately withheld. "Sometimes I feel that the account executive is not completely open with our workgroup, for whatever reason. I really don't have an explanation for that, but it just seems that a lot of communication is kept hidden from us."

One survey participant who works for a large pharmaceutical company said he was shocked when he realized that "75 percent of the time when I go visit somebody, I unwittingly transmit information that is valuable to that person's work . . . I'll come up and just say something or I'll mention that I saw a fax go by that said this and that, or the business process improvement that I'm working on is doing such and such and they'll say 'Really, how come Finance didn't find out about this?' And it happens daily!" The reason is that his boss gathers and hoards information, and then releases it when it's most advantageous to him.

"But it can be too late for other people to react, it can be too slow," he noted. "If my boss got hit by a truck today he would leave a big problem because he's one of the few people who knows some of the situations."

The same boss also is a master at letting new ideas die. "One of the very effective techniques he has is to say 'Let me think about it for a few days. . . . ' And another week would go by and it would be the same thing. . . . You could end up stonewalled for months that way if you're not careful."

If I were able to ask that boss whether he was intentionally inhibiting performance, he would certainly say no. I have never talked with a single leader who said that he or she sets out to stifle performance, lose money, or sap the morale of the workforce. However, by micromanaging, hoarding information, and acting in their own best interest, that is exactly what they are doing.

In Chapter 7, I'll highlight some companies that *are* behaving in an intentional way—they are deliberately creating environments where high performance can flourish. These companies are building senior management teams that are themselves high-performing workgroups and are models for the rest of the company. From the CEO on down, these companies are fostering high-performance environments and achieving profitable growth.

## Key Points

- The behaviors mentioned most frequently in our study that extinguish thinking are micromanaging, hoarding information, and leaders acting in their own self-interest.
- Short-term focus is killing performance. Our research found that members of both high-performing *and* nonperforming groups feel overworked and at the mercy of short-term goals.
- The way companies are cutting costs—and how deep they are cutting—is affecting their ability to grow profitably.

## Unexpected Findings

- Nearly 40 percent of respondents in the study could offer no evidence that their workgroups were doing something tangible to contribute to the company's performance.
- Almost one-third of the respondents in nonperforming workgroups classified their groups as used-to-be's, i.e., they were high performing in the past but are no longer.

# CHAPTER 7

# Results the Right Way

This book is about spreading high performance throughout your organization. For most companies, that means increasing the performance of your top
workgroups and moving the middle—putting members of
high-performing groups together with the almost-
there's to improve both groups. However, some organizations deliberately set out to achieve a company-wide
high-performance environment from the outset.

Our research identified companies that not only have a
firm grasp of how they fit in to the evolving economy but
also understand the link between the internal environment and sustainable growth. Among them are publicly
traded corporations, professional services firms, and
family-owned businesses. Many of their senior leaders are
baby boomers who have realized, after years in negative
environments, that there is a better way to run a company—
and make more money at the same time. "I'm amazed that
people don't understand that your corporate culture is

what differentiates you long term," said Tom Mendoza, president of Network Appliance.

Support for high performance from the top is more unusual than you might think. One of the most interesting findings of the Hudson Highland Center for High Performance study is that only 58 percent of respondents said their company supports high performance. That compares to 70 percent who said that their group leader does so.

Not surprisingly, a larger percentage of respondents in high-performing workgroups said that they get corporate support (75 percent) and group leader support (84 percent) than those in average-performing and nonperforming groups. The gap between corporate and group leader support is smallest in the high-performing groups and largest in nonperforming groups. These findings imply that high performance is enhanced when the group leader and the company both support the group.

Network Appliance, Macquarie Capital Partners, The Beryl Companies, SRA International, and Bright Horizons were among the companies that stood out in our research because they deliberately created high-performance work environments.

## Network Appliance

Network Appliance is a highly successful company that understands the importance of valuing people. Senior leaders hire very smart people and expect them to find ways to make an impact. Employees are given goals but are not told how to accomplish them. They have access to the information they need to make good decisions and grow the business. Workers are encouraged to take risks and are not punished for failure.

When they suggest a new idea, it is considered seriously, Mendoza said. "Even if people decide that it's not a good idea, it's discussed and thought through. . . . Many of our best strategies come from a lot of bright people who don't have any kind of title," he added.

Network Appliance, a world leader in unified storage solutions, became profitable in 1996. The company had 21 consecutive quarters with more than 70 percent year-over-year revenue growth, beginning with its initial public offering in November 1995. Fiscal 2003 revenues were $892 million. NetApp has made the list of *Fortune* magazine's "100 Best Companies to Work For" for the past two years.

There is no question that NetApp means business. "Everybody wants to be nice to each other, but at the end of the day, we believe corporate cultures are built on winning," Mendoza noted. "We have extraordinarily high expectations of ourselves."

Mendoza encourages employees to think. He tells new employees, "You are now working for the greatest company on earth. We're going to listen to you. Here's how we're different than most companies: We expect an impact out of you now."

The company shows respect for its employees by giving them every opportunity to do well. "We believe that you have to apply the principle of fairness—did we explain [the task] correctly, did we give them the opportunity, did we help them? If they can't measure up, we've got to put somebody else in that job and we've got to run faster."

NetApp believes in articulating a vision that people can understand and act on. "We hire motivated people and then we help create an environment they want to run through a wall for," Mendoza said. "If you really want to have a 'run-through-the-wall' attitude, you have to believe that you are creating a company that will do something very special," he added.

Once a month, executives hold "brown bag" lunches in which they meet with a group of about twenty employees to answer questions and listen to any concerns they might have about the company. Those who attend are asked to go back and share what they heard with their coworkers. "We have eight guys doing [the brown bags], so these get done a lot. I do it everywhere I go in the world . . . I'll sit there and answer anything they want to hear."

Network Appliance has a long tradition of recognizing every sales win throughout the company. Those who made the sale pass on information about the customer and recognize the people who helped them. "You know what [being recognized] does to the morale of the person who got on a plane late at night or worked on a proposal," Mendoza commented.

While leadership is important at NetApp, hierarchy isn't. No one in the company has an office; everyone, including Mendoza and CEO Dan Warmenhoven, has a cubicle. "It's an environment of management by walking around, which is the only way to go," Mendoza said.

Senior managers encourage people to make decisions, and make them quickly. "We believe it's much better to move faster than everybody else than it is to debate the topic for too long," Mendoza said. The company also recognizes and rewards good ideas, regardless of who comes up with them. "We believe that there are very few all right and all wrong answers to anything, and we would much rather that the employee's idea be the one you take."

There is nothing "soft" about how NetApp is run. As Mendoza put it, "I'm not a 'hug a tree' guy." The company gets results, and it gets them the right way.

## Macquarie Capital Partners

Macquarie Capital Partners deliberately set out to build an environment different from other investment banks. Most investment banks foster an attitude of "each man for himself." At Macquarie, leaders have created an environment that encourages collaboration. The goal is for the best minds to work toward a common goal.

"We wanted to do something that had not been done before," explained Don Suter, managing principal.

Recognizing that the business requires long hours and enormous commitment, "We wanted to create an environment where the people you work with become your extended family. You actually look forward to coming into work every day because of the people, the intellectual stimulation of what you're doing, and the feeling of collegiality in the office."

In addition, "face time" is not valued at Macquarie. Employees are encouraged to spend time with their families and have a life outside the office. "It really takes as long as six to twelve months to reprogram people. The younger ones are accustomed to thinking 'If I'm any good, if I'm going to make something of myself here, I've got to put in a hundred hours a week.' "

While it is a young company, Macquarie is recognized as one of the elite firms globally in its primary business of helping real estate companies raise private equity. The company spends about 30 percent of its time doing financial advisory work for real estate clients. Founded in January 2001, the thirty-five-member firm has principal offices in Chicago and London. It has been profitable each year since its inception, and generated a record $25 million in revenue in fiscal 2003.

Macquarie Capital Partners is owned by its employees, in partnership with Macquarie Bank, Australia's largest independent investment bank. The members of the management team worked together at Security Capital Group prior to forming their own firm.

Suter noted that investment bankers typically are among the best and brightest in the financial services industry. They work extremely hard, are highly motivated, and deliver very high-quality work. However, there is a flip side.

"On the negative side, the things that people will say about investment bankers are that they're arrogant, they're greedy, they're only doing it for the money, they're very short-term focused, they'll run over the person in the office next to them if they think it would give them a larger bonus this year. And generally speaking, you can never turn your back on one of them, even if they're your colleague."

Suter and his partners believe that the reason Wall Street investment bankers behave the way that they do is because of how they're rewarded. "If you pay individuals bonuses for grabbing control of a deal and taking credit for other people's work . . . they will do it," he said.

Consequently, at Macquarie, there is one set of short-term financial objectives for the year that covers everyone in the company. "Everyone helps each other because they get paid to behave that way. You get rewarded at the end of the year based on whether our company met its financial objectives," Suter said.

Christopher Vallace, a principal in the company, added, "We're judged as to how we do as a unified company as opposed to individuals. It's not a me-first attitude. . . . Everyone wants to achieve their own individual targets. But I'd say that's secondary to the long-term success of the firm."

Associates and above are given an ownership stake after a few years with the company. In addition to salary, employees are compensated with three types of incentives. "We've organized the compensation here in a way that is 100 percent supportive and consistent with the type of culture we're trying to build," Suter said. "In order to build the business you have got to have everybody thinking the way you think. You can't have one person sitting in the corner office thinking one way and everybody else thinking a different way."

So far, the strategy is paying off. Not only is the company making money, but Macquarie Capital Partners is a place people want to work. The investment bankers could go anywhere, but they choose to stay. "They all get offers and they don't leave because, at the end of the day, no matter what people say, it's not just about the money," Suter said.

"I am one of the few people who absolutely loves what they do. And I think if you called up everybody who works in this company they would tell you the same thing. . . . The people here feel like there is nothing that we can't accomplish, and that is what gives all of us this sense of excitement for the future."

## The Beryl Companies

From the beginning, The Beryl Companies, a family-owned call center business, has created an environment that puts those on the front line first. Call advisers—the people who pick up the phone—are at the top of the organization chart and everyone else is there to support them.

Call advisers function in self-directed teams. "We find that many times that can be as effective, if not more effective, than a hierarchical structure where they're reporting to someone who is telling them how to do things," said CEO Paul Spiegelman.

"There is no bureaucracy here," said one employee. "We are free to communicate however and with whomever we need to in order to get our jobs done. We do not cling to rules for rules' sake, but instead make sure that what we are doing makes sense for the job at hand."

Founded in Texas in 1985, the company provides information and referrals to consumers to connect them with appropriate health-care resources. Spiegelman and his two brothers started the business for a personal reason. Their grandfather, who had congestive heart failure, was in and out of the hospital. The brothers recognized the need for a service that would transport elderly and sick people to the hospital.

"What's driven us to this day is the fact that we provide a very human service that affects people's lives. . . . And even though we sold our original business, that philosophy, that goal, has remained the same," said Spiegelman. Today, Beryl has about $15 million in annual sales and employs 225 people.

While the brothers "fell into" the call center business, they very deliberately decided how they wanted to relate to their employees. They chose to remain small so that they could maintain their values and hire people who shared them.

Spiegelman stresses The Beryl Companies' three values at every opportunity—a passion for customer service, always doing the right thing, and never sacrificing quality. "It's just been amazing to me what an impact these have had. I'll be sitting in meetings and people will bring up 'What about that value, does it meet that value?'"

At Beryl, creating the right environment starts by hiring the right people. "In our recruiting process we talk about hiring the heart, not the head. We're not looking for someone who's got basic computer experience, we're looking for someone who has compassion and has that innate sense of wanting to help people," Spiegelman said.

The company places a great deal of emphasis on customer service and training. New hires go through four or five weeks of training before they ever pick up a call, and they receive ongoing training weekly. The combination of training and the employee's innate personality "makes the impression upon the caller and ultimately builds our reputation and builds our business," he added. Employees get a monthly report card, which focuses not on what they are doing wrong but on what they are doing right.

Turnover at Beryl is extremely low compared to other call centers. When Spiegelman sends a personal note card to employees each year on their anniversary, "I'm writing notes for people who have been here four years, five years, six years, which is kind of unheard of in the call center industry. That's pretty neat to see," he said.

As a result of the way Beryl treats people, it was named one of the top ten midsize places to work in the Dallas/Fort Worth market by the *Dallas Business Journal* in 2003. That recognition is not surprising, given the positive feelings employees have about the company. Said one call center adviser, "We are the best in our industry. [There is] nothing like being on a winning team to make you feel good!" Added another, "Being in the health-care industry, we feel we're called to a higher purpose; there's the feeling that what you do every day really does matter."

## SRA International

SRA International is a Fairfax, Virginia—based information technology services company. Building the right work environment was critical to the company's founders.

"We actually got to create this business. We had a clean sheet of paper and you don't get to do that very often," said Chief Operating Officer Ted Legasey, who has been with the company since its inception in 1978. "We got to make all the rules, we got to set the values, we chose what we were going to emphasize with our employees, and then we created a culture around that."

From the beginning, the company's leaders have espoused three essential attributes: honesty, customer satisfaction, and caring about people. In addition to strong core values, SRA understands the marketplace well. In the last several years, as the commercial market for IT services dried up, SRA increased its business with the federal government from 80 to 100 percent.

"All of a sudden the federal market space became attractive to the public markets. So those of us who had been in this marketplace for quite some time said, 'Let's sharpen our focus even more crisply and become, in the parlance of the market, a pure play,'" Legasey said.

The decision was ratified on Wall Street. "We did our IPO in May 2002 at $18. We did a secondary [offering] in June 2003, thirteen months later, at $30," Legasey noted. "We grew revenues every year we were in business; we made a profit every quarter we were in business." Sales in 2003 were $450 million, according to Hoover's.

The company has been on the *Fortune* list of "100 Best Companies to Work For" for five consecutive years. If you ask employees about the environment, "they will tell you that they get to work in a company where their opinion matters. People will listen to them. . . . They don't have to worry about anybody stabbing them in the back. They get to work in a collaborative environment where people are uniformly cooperating with each other," Legasey said.

SRA understands the importance of giving knowledge workers the chance to think. "For knowledge workers, if they're not getting to work on things that really resonate with their professional ambitions, with the substantive areas that they're interested in, they're going to get bored. They're going to get distracted, they're going to go looking for something else," Legasey said.

Job content and the company values are at the center of SRA's model for the environment it seeks to achieve. Surrounding the core are leadership, career opportunities, and work environment (defined as things such as the hours people work, their commuting time, and the amount of travel they have to do).

Explaining the company's definition of leadership, Legasey said, "The leadership piece is a working environment where people see their leaders as really enabling them to do more than they ever thought they'd be able to do by themselves." The final factor in the model is compensation. Legasey noted that the key is for all six pieces to be in balance.

"If we manage ourselves well, we will put the numbers up on the scoreboard," he said. "The financial performance is an output, it's an outcome from doing the right job for the customers and for treating the employees correctly."

## Bright Horizons

Linda Mason and Roger Brown, a husband and wife team, built a highly successful workplace child-care center business founded on the principle that child-care workers should be treated with respect.

Recognizing the demand for work site child care as a way for employers to attract and retain employees, the couple built Bright Horizons Family Solutions, Inc., from a start-up with four employees to sixteen thousand workers at five hundred centers operating in thirty-seven states and four countries. One of the largest independent providers of workplace child care in the United States, the publicly owned company had $472.8 million in revenues in 2003. Clients include more than eighty Fortune 500 companies.

Before founding the business in 1986, Mason and Brown spent several years doing famine relief work in Sudan and Ethiopia. They quickly created a large national operation to provide food to 400,000 people. They also ran refugee camps in eastern Sudan. As managers in Africa, and earlier as relief workers in Cambodia, the couple saw firsthand the effects that lack of professionalism, very low pay, and inadequate management can have on a workforce. "There was tremendous burnout and turnover," Mason recalled. She and her husband focused on treating workers respectfully, instituting training programs and professional development, which in turn led to a high level of esprit de corps.

"When we came back to the United States and started investigating child care, we saw the parallels—undervalued employees suffering from a lack of professionalism, high burnout, and turnover," Mason said. "We decided to turn the approach on its head and create a different kind of an organization." The company would be centered around a high-caliber faculty that would provide quality child care and have opportunities for professional growth in a network of workplace centers.

One of the first things Bright Horizons did was to write a mission statement setting forth six organizational values: respect, nurturing, trust, openness to change, balance, and sustainability.

Following through on its commitment to professional growth, Bright Horizons provides training and education that can lead to a degree in early childhood education. Employees can begin as assistants and become teachers, head teachers, directors, and regional managers. "We have a tremendous history of people being developed from within," Mason said. About 40 percent of the faculty are professionals with bachelor's or associate's degrees in early childhood education or psychology. Another group of employees are empty nesters, primarily mature mothers who have experience with children but no degree in early childhood education. The third category of workers are entry-level people who aren't yet degreed or who have changed fields.

Center directors are smart people who are treated like smart people. They are given a great deal of autonomy to run the center to meet the needs of the local community. "We try to limit the number of things that central management imposes or requires. We want the director to take ownership of the center. I tell directors, 'I want your center to be your center,'" Mason said. The company has strong control of quality standards, equipment and supplies, and the overarching philosophy of meeting children's developmental, emotional, social, physical, and intellectual needs. Beyond that, how the director develops the center reflects who she is and the parents she serves.

Best practices developed by individual centers are promulgated throughout the organization. A task force made up of teachers, called Better Together, comes together to discuss best practices that make a great work environment.

Employees are recognized for achievement, and the management style is collegial and nonhierarchical. For example, if a teacher has devised an interesting curriculum for a certain unit, the company celebrates it by putting it in the newsletter, or on the Intranet. "We have a strong focus on excellence. People work hard and have fun," noted Mason.

The company has been a leader in allowing flexible work hours. Part-time work and job sharing are among the options for employees. It also demonstrates respect for employees by paying teachers 20 percent more than the market average, as well as providing extensive benefits. Bright Horizons made *Fortune* magazine's list of "100 Best Companies to Work For in America" five times, including 2004.

While other major chains of child-care centers have stagnated or gone through bankruptcy during the last half dozen years, Bright Horizons has continued to grow. Mason attributes this to the company's focus on high quality, and the fact that no other chain does employer-supported child care.

"Child care is a business issue for employees," Mason said. "Companies are hiring women in great numbers, but lose them after they have babies because they can't find adequate child care. The biggest source of turnover is child-care problems." Studies have shown that companies are able to pay for child-care centers in their first year through saved recruiting and training costs. "[Quality child care] cuts the turnover of a vulnerable class of employees by half," Mason added.

Another reason for Bright Horizon's growth is that onsite child-care centers are a draw for parents who understand the importance of the first five years to their children's development. "Once a major employer has onsite child-care centers, its competitors have to have that too. When we get a major player in the insurance industry, for example, we approach all their competitors," Mason said.

The company's market has exploded, as major corporations open fifteen or twenty centers. "Our base of who we can draw from is limitless. Less than ten percent of major corporations have a child-care center," Mason said. Bright Horizons also markets to universities, the government, hospitals, and other major employers.

The company also has been able to grow because its capital needs are minimal. Employers build the centers and pay for equipping them. While the company is profitable, "we do not target to have a high profit margin. The bulk of our costs are personnel," Mason explained. Bright Horizons seeks high quality and high growth, and it has achieved both.

All of the companies described above have achieved impressive financial results and created an environment in which people are valued, have the latitude to think, and are encouraged to seize opportunities. These companies get financial results the right way. They are not afraid to defy conventional wisdom, and they are likely to sustain profitable growth. In the concluding chapter, I will debunk the conventional wisdom and share the ten most important lessons I have learned from our research.

## Key Points

- Our research identified companies that not only have a firm grasp of how they fit into the evolving economy but understand the link between the internal environment and sustainable growth. Among them are publicly traded corporations, professional services firms, and family-owned businesses.

- One of the most interesting findings of the Hudson Highland Center for High Performance study is that only 58 percent of respondents said their company supports high performance. That compares to 70 percent who said that their group leader does so.

- A larger percentage of respondents in high-performing workgroups said that they get corporate support (75 percent) and group leader support (84 percent) than those in average-performing and nonperforming groups.

- The gap between corporate and group leader support is smallest in the high-performing groups and largest in nonperforming groups.

- These findings imply that high performance is enhanced when the group leader and the company both support the group.

# CHAPTER 8

# Defying Conventional Wisdom

Conventional wisdom isn't getting companies where they want to be. In this chapter, I will summarize the ten most important lessons I have learned in the course of researching this book. They all defy conventional wisdom. If you embrace these lessons, you will be well on your way to creating a high-performance environment.

No matter where in the world your company is, the drivers of high performance are the same. Knowing your business and meeting your customers' needs are important, but they are not enough. What drives high performance is valuing people, optimizing critical thinking, and seizing opportunities. Without an environment in which these occur, your company will not be able to develop the new products, services, or markets you need to sustain profitable growth.

## 1. Short-Term Thinking Kills Performance

The emphasis on quarterly results has never been greater. Ironically, our research shows that the number one inhibitor of high performance is short-term thinking—living for today at the expense of tomorrow. To meet quarterly financial goals, companies are cutting staff and budgets, resulting in overworked, frustrated employees.

On the day they announced their IPO, the founders of Google vowed to concentrate on the long term. "In our opinion, outside pressures too often tempt companies to sacrifice long-term opportunities to meet quarterly market expectations. . . . If opportunities arise that might cause us to sacrifice short-term results but are in the best long-term interest of our shareholders, we will take those opportunities. We will have the fortitude to do this. We would request that our shareholders take the long-term view," wrote Larry Page and Sergey Brin. To spawn the creativity that leads to opportunities, Google encourages employees to spend 20 percent of their time working on whatever they think will most benefit the company in the long run.

Balancing the short and long term is perhaps the single biggest challenge facing companies today. Not all senior leaders have the fortitude to sacrifice short-term results. However, all do have the opportunity to collaborate with their workgroups to attain an intelligent balance. Yet too often senior leaders try to accomplish this difficult task on their own. They make across-the-board cuts without looking at how these decisions affect the individual workgroup. Far too little input comes from outside the executive board room.

Senior leaders need to engage members of high-performing workgroups in discussions about the challenges facing the company and the financial targets the company proposes for the workgroup. Are the goals achievable? How will meeting the targets affect future as well as current performance? Once senior management and the workgroup leader agree on realistic targets, the group should decide how to achieve them. There are different ways to get to the same place. Across-the-board cuts may not be the answer.

### 2. The Leader Protects the Group from Company Interference

The Hudson Highland Center for High Performance research found that one of the biggest differentiators between high-performing and nonperforming workgroups is that the leaders of high-performing groups protect the group from the larger company "so that we can do our work." The research implies that, in too many companies, protection is a necessary condition of high performance. The leader is forced to put time and energy into combating the interference, often in highly imaginative and resourceful ways. One leader I met recently who spends a great deal of time protecting his group calls his behavior "intelligent disobedience." Imagine if this intelligence, ingenuity, and energy were put into positive pursuits!

When I teach executive education classes at the University of Chicago Graduate School of Business and INSEAD in Fontainebleau, France, I begin my classes with the research results. The students in these classes are handpicked by their companies as high performers. Most are leaders of essential workgroups in their companies. When I talk about how the leader is a buffer between the company and his workgroup, many heads nod in agreement. Inevitably, people come up to me after class to say, "No wonder I am so exhausted, since I spend so much time and energy combating interference."

Typically, a month or two after class ends, I get a call or an e-mail from one of these students saying he or she has decided to move on. The student usually says something like, "I couldn't take it anymore. I quit my job and I never felt better." Recently, I got a call from one of my executive MBA students. She had left the company where she worked for twenty years to start her own business. She saw her former company as shortsighted and risk averse. Management tried to convince her to stay, but more money and a better title didn't solve her problem. She wanted an environment that fully utilized her brain, and decided to create it on her own.

More often than not, these students don't quit their jobs because they have another position. They just want out.

These are the risk takers—those willing to challenge the status quo to find a better way to do things. They are the leaders most likely to drive high performance. They are exactly the kind of people that companies should develop and nurture, yet the companies are inadvertently driving them out. No senior leadership team deliberately sets out to decrease the performance of its best workgroups. However, that is exactly what is happening. It's time for top managers to start removing barriers that are forcing leaders to spend more time protecting their high-performing workgroups than making money for the company.

### 3. Productivity Plus Innovation Drive High Performance

There is an important difference between productivity and high performance, although the two concepts are often used interchangeably. I suspect that is why 77 percent of the respondents in our study said that they consider their workgroup to be a high-performing unit within their company, when only 10 percent could provide evidence that this was so.

In recent years, some economists have argued that relying on productivity numbers to measure performance is misleading and potentially counterproductive. Based on an industrial model, productivity is still calculated as the number of units produced in a given period of time by a worker. But in a knowledge-based economy in which the service sector employs 80 percent of the workforce, productivity is much more difficult to measure. In addition, the ubiquity of e-mail, cell phones, laptop computers, and other communication technology makes it possible for professional and managerial workers to work from their cars, their homes, and even the beach—and those hours are not captured when measuring productivity.

Managers who solely emphasize productivity tend to drive out the capacity in their workers to engage in innovation and creativity. Knowledge workers, by definition, cannot provide full value to their organization simply through productivity increases. To increase shareholder value and sustain profitability, companies should foster creativity. Innovation combined with productivity leads to high performance.

### 4. It's the Environment, Not the Leader

Our research demonstrates that the workgroup environment, not the leader, is the most important factor in driving high performance. This is true across industries and geographies. There is no single personality or style that defines an effective leader. What these leaders have in common is the ability to create an environment that values people (treating smart people as if they are smart), optimizes critical thinking (minimizing emotional responses by matching words and actions), and seizes opportunities (creating learning environments that turn challenges into opportunities). They create environments where people want to go to work every day.

Too often, high performance is dependent on a leader

who intuitively understands the need for this environment. This leaves high performance to chance. The problem is that when the leader leaves, the group loses its ability to achieve peak performance. Companies can stop dependence on the leader by making the group responsible for creating a high-performance environment.

One way to do this is to conduct a 360-degree feedback process to evaluate the environment, gathering input from the group's leader, members, and customers, as well as other workgroups with whom it interacts. The group should discuss what it can start, continue, or stop doing to drive business results and make the workgroup something people really want to be a part of.

## 5. *It's the Workgroup, Not the Individual*

Individual performance is important, but it is affected by the environment. You can put your very best workers in the wrong environment, and they will not do their best work.

It is important for companies to develop high-potential individuals by providing training and mentoring and by helping them plan a career path. But if you want to get the biggest return on your human capital investment, make sure these individuals are in a high-performing workgroup. In our study, we found not only that talented individuals thrive in high-performance environments but such environments also increase the likelihood of B players becoming A players.

Even stars need to be able to function well in the work-group. If you have people in your company who care more about looking good than helping the group look good; if they do only what will advance their own careers; if they define "winning" as beating their teammates, they will destroy the high-performance environment. High-performing work-groups accept that "we are in this together." They realize that the whole is greater than the sum of its parts.

To maximize performance, the leader needs to leverage the skills of group members by playing to their strengths—not only their functional skills but also their natural abilities. Who is the go-to person for evaluating downside risk? Who is best at seeing upside potential? Who is the one who knows the historical context of a current situation? Taking advantage of differing skills enhances the group's ability to collaborate effectively.

### 6. There Is Room to Grow

Even the highest-performing workgroups in our study could do better. In fact, the easiest, most efficient way to increase the overall performance of your company is to increase the performance of those groups already at the top by encouraging group members to speak the unspeakable, pass the ball to the right player, and practice respectful communication.

Ironically, rather than helping high-performing groups do better, companies often force them to do more with less. They say "you did this so well with eight people that we're going to cut you down to six." They tamper with these groups until they are no longer high performing.

Another way to increase overall performance is by moving average-performing workgroups into the high-performing category. By instituting a process for high- and average-performing groups to collaborate on solving problems and overcoming barriers, you can increase the overall performance of your company.

## 7. *Your Employees Can Solve Your Problems*

The first thing companies often do when they confront a serious challenge is to hire a team of consultants. While consultants can provide valuable insight from the viewpoint of outsiders, I would suggest that the first thing companies should do is consult their own employees. Because employees know the company well, they usually can figure out how to solve the problem.

For this to work, you first need to offer "amnesty" to employees for telling the truth about what needs to be done. Promise them that they will face no negative consequences for offering their ideas. The reason they don't come to you in the first place is that they fear they will be at the top of the list when the next downsizing occurs.

I have shared the results of my research on high performance with many audiences around the world. At an event in Japan, a young man came up to me after my presentation and told me the following story. He said that he worked for a manufacturing company that was trying to reduce cycle time. The company had engaged three strategy consulting firms to solve the problem to no avail. Management decided to hold a contest and sent out a "Request for Proposal" to the internal staff. His workgroup responded and got the assignment. The group members were afraid of offending the company's leaders by challenging some existing practices so they asked a senior-level manager to coach them about how to best approach management. With the coach's help, they were able to respectfully suggest ways to solve the problem. Senior management listened, and the group accomplished the goal.

While the type of coaching the group received is difficult to find, the bigger problem is that many companies don't ever turn to their own employees when they need smart thinking.

## 8. The "Dumb" Idea Could Be the Next Paradigm Shift

The next time one of your workgroups comes to you with a "dumb" idea, ask yourself whether it's really a bad idea, or whether it represents a paradigm shift that you don't grasp. You may be rejecting innovative ways to differentiate your company and move it forward because the ideas sound foreign to you. Remember that new ideas always do.

The workers coming into companies today see the world differently than their bosses. The new generation has never known life without a computer. They are fluent in the language of new technology, having spoken it since they were very young. They want to use technology to open up new opportunities.

While today's senior managers have the experience to take new ideas and make them work, they did not grow up speaking the language of new technology. Consequently, the best they can do is translate. They think, "How can we use technology to do the same thing we used to do, but better, faster, and cheaper?" As a result, companies are digitizing many processes they used to do manually. While this is necessary, it is not enough. Sustaining profitable growth depends on using technology to invent new opportunities.

Companies need to stop and listen to the "dumb" new ideas. Looking for what's wrong with these ideas—whether they come from the executive boardroom, the newest hire, or the janitor—is a dangerous strategy in a diverse and changing world. Instead, you need to look for what's smart about new ideas, since they are the future of your company.

### 9. *Workers Need More Information, Not Less*

Although companies hire knowledge workers for their ability to think, they often don't give these workers the information they need to do their best work. Senior managers shield workers from information they believe will scare them. They hoard information they are afraid the competition will use against them. Of course, companies do these things with good intentions. Unfortunately, it is counterproductive.

Companies would do well to learn from the experience

of Tom Mendoza, president of Network Appliance, who was advised not to give all the facts to his employees. He didn't listen. Instead, he gave employees the information they needed to build a successful company. And the employees stayed.

In high-performing groups, workers have the information they need to do their jobs. They are told where the company needs to go, the problems it faces, and what keeps senior leaders up at night. They are challenged to use this information to push the company ahead. They don't let fear of the competition get in the way of progress. Most importantly, they trust their employees to use the information in the company's best interest. When you treat people as though they are smart and trustworthy, most will prove you right.

### 10. *Build It and They Will Come . . . and Stay*

High-performing groups are talent magnets. Perhaps your company's reputation, or your compensation plan, or the job description got talented employees in the door, but those factors won't keep them. The ability to work in a high-performance environment is what makes your employees stay.

Top performers like to be challenged intellectually and given responsibility for results. They like to be told what the goal is, not how to achieve it. They don't want to work in an environment where information is withheld, or where leaders pursue a personal agenda.

After conducting in-depth interviews with highly paid and well-educated knowledge workers from companies all over the world, it became clear to me that most companies are not creating the environments that will keep their best employees. Respondents told countless stories about how their company was stifling the workgroup's performance. They said they were waiting for the job market to open up so they could get another job. Unfortunately, until more companies build the right environment, there will not be enough places for these frustrated workers to go.

## Conclusion

Rejecting conventional wisdom is not easy. It takes courage to try something new. It takes courage to sacrifice short-term results to attain more significant long-term goals. It takes courage to eliminate the interference that forces workgroup leaders to protect their groups. It takes courage to trust that the people in your company have the secrets to success and to allow them to share those secrets throughout your organization. And, most importantly, it takes courage to listen, ask questions, allow failure, and keep learning.

I hope that this book will make it easier. By examining the hard evidence our study provides and learning the lessons of the workgroups and companies that have done it right, I hope you will be able to muster the courage to move forward.

This book is written for you, whether you are the CEO of a major company, head of a business unit, leader of a workgroup—or aspire to any of these positions. The message is very simple. To be a winner, you need to achieve results the right way. Once you do that, success is contagious.

*Conventional Wisdom Versus Reality*

| Conventional Wisdom | Reality |
| --- | --- |
| Meeting quarterly goals is a measure of success. | Short-term thinking kills performance. |
| Company and workgroup leaders partner to achieve high performance. | The leader protects the group from company interference. |
| Productivity equals high performance. | Productivity plus innovation drive high performance. |
| The leader is the most important factor in achieving a high-performing workgroup. | It's the environment, not the leader. |

| Conventional Wisdom | Reality |
| --- | --- |
| Hiring and nurturing high-potential individuals will drive high performance. | It's the workgroup not the individual. |
| The best way to improve performance is to eliminate low-performing groups. | Even top-performing groups have room to grow. |
| If you're facing a tough challenge, get outside help. | Your employees can solve your problems. |
| You can grow profitably by finding what's wrong with an idea and trying to fix it. | The "dumb" idea could be the next paradigm shift. |
| Companies should withhold information so the competition doesn't get it. | Workers need more information, not less, to do their jobs well. |
| To retain top employees, give them the right salary, benefits, and training. | Build the right environment and they will come . . . and stay. |

# Conducting the Study

The Hudson Highland Center for High Performance global study, conducted in conjunction with Richard Day Research of Evanston, Illinois, examined knowledge workers from around the world to determine what affects high performance in workgroups.

The study is distinguished by its scope and breadth compared to other studies, and the rigor with which it was conducted. The Center and Richard Day Research developed a research design to systematically reach the greatest number of knowledge workers ever contacted for one study.

## Survey Participants—Eligibility Criteria

To qualify as a knowledge worker for the purposes of the study, respondents had to possess the following demographic characteristics:

- Current employment: full-time managerial, professional, or technical
- Education: minimum of U.S. bachelor's degree or equivalent
- Income: minimum top decile in their country

They also had to agree that their job included at least three of the following five tasks:

- Reviewing and interpreting information
- Developing new ideas and insights
- Continual learning about their area of expertise
- A significant amount of independent thought, rather than following others' directions
- Using information to develop or refine products or processes

Further, knowledge workers who took part in the study had to work for specific types of organizations. In the United States, their employers had to be:

- Publicly traded companies listed on a stock exchange or bourse
- Large professional services companies (accounting, legal, consulting, financial, or brokerage services with one hundred or more professionals)

For knowledge workers in Europe, Asia, and Australia, the range of organizations was expanded to include three additional categories:

- Private companies with ten thousand or more employees
- Joint ventures involving a government and a private company that produce a commercial product or service (e.g., German rail)
- Government agencies that produce a commercial product or service (e.g., health system)

## Data Collection

The study includes responses from 3,104 knowledge workers around the world. It was conducted in two phases.

### Phase One: United States

The first phase involved 1,015 knowledge workers in the United States. Respondents were drawn from an online panel of more than one million people maintained by Greenfield Online, a Connecticut-based Internet research organization. The panel closely mirrors the U.S. population but skews toward higher than average education and income levels.

E-mail invitations were sent to panel members who,

based on available demographic information, appeared most likely to fit the profile of a knowledge worker. Respondents were screened using the criteria described above. Those who qualified as knowledge workers completed the online survey.

More than twenty thousand panel members attempted to take the knowledge worker survey. Of that number, 1,015 (slightly more than 5 percent) qualified and went on to complete the survey.

Subsequently, Richard Day Research conducted telephone interviews with 592 of those respondents. Those interviews lasted approximately thirty minutes.

Finally, in-depth follow-up interviews were conducted with a smaller subset in 2003.

### Phase Two: Global Study

The second phase involved 2,089 knowledge workers in Europe, Asia, and Australia. Countries and regions included in phase two were:

| Country | Number of Interviews |
|---|---|
| United Kingdom | 307 |
| Germany | 265 |
| France | 278 |
| Italy | 89 |
| Sweden | 164 |
| Netherlands | 187 |

| Country | Number of Interviews |
|---|---|
| Japan | 294 |
| China (Beijing/Shanghai) | 291 |
| Australia | 214 |

These countries were selected because they were known to have relatively large numbers of knowledge workers. The goal was to collect a sufficient number of interviews to obtain a global cross section of different types of knowledge workers.

For phase two, the project team decided to rely entirely on Internet surveys to collect data. That decision was made primarily because alternative methods would have been cost- and time-prohibitive, and more subject to local variation in implementation. Experience during the U.S. phase of the study demonstrated that the Internet is well suited for communicating with the highly educated, technically adept knowledge workers the team was seeking.

China presented a number of challenges, including the limited availability of Internet panelists. As a result, the project team decided to confine the survey to Beijing and Shanghai, two of China's largest and most important cities. All references to China are therefore based on data from those two cities and not the entire country.

The project team called on Munich-based Ciao AG and its worldwide network of partner companies to implement the global survey in phase two. Ciao employees translated the questionnaire from U.S. business English into the requisite languages. RDR then had native speakers retranslate them to ensure they were idiomatic while remaining consistent with the original English questionnaire.

Data collection took place in October 2003. As in the U.S. phase, potential participants received e-mail invitations. Those who fit the knowledge worker profile—between 5 percent and 19 percent of respondents, depending on the country—went on to take the survey.

## Regional Analysis and Weighting

Because responses from the six European countries included in the study were relatively uniform, they were grouped together as Europe. The other regions—the United States, Japan, Beijing/Shanghai, and Australia— were examined individually.

To derive a single, global measurement, the project team weighted the data to reflect the relative proportion of knowledge workers in each participating country/region. The team reviewed labor force and census data from national and international sources, then estimated the total number of knowledge workers in each country and assigned weights accordingly. The weights are educated guesses reflecting the best judgment of the team—China presented formidable difficulties—and other researchers could have arrived at different estimates.

## Questionnaire

### Measuring High Performance

There are many ways to define high performance. The research study employed the following definition: "(Your workgroup is high performing if it) adapts to changing conditions and consistently exceeds performance goals and the performance of its peer groups." That definition grew out of a review of research literature and the experience of the project team.

Knowledge workers were asked to assess their workgroup using the definition. However, the research team did not rely on self-assessment alone: Knowledge workers also were asked to provide more objective evidence of high performance—profit growth, revenue growth, process innovation, product/service innovation, social responsibility, customer satisfaction or recognition from clients, safety, teamwork, or something else. Based on that information, each respondent's workgroup was categorized as high performing, average performing, or nonperforming.

To be included among the high-performing workgroups, respondents had to provide evidence of profit and/or revenue growth, as well as product, service, or process innovation.

### Performance Scorecard

In phase one, U.S. knowledge workers completed a seventeen-question Performance Scorecard. The questions were compiled following an extensive literature review, and reflected the project team's collective assessment of the attributes that drive high performance.

For the second phase, the project team refined the Performance Scorecard and expanded it to forty-seven items. Some items were identical to the original questions, while some were revised and many new ones were added. A group of respondents from the original U.S. survey also completed the expanded Performance Scorecard to determine whether their responses on both were consistent. Comparing the results indicated that the new questions were as effective as the earlier ones in differentiating between high and low performance.

### Open-Ended Questions

As noted above, a subset of the participants in the U.S. phase of the study—592 out of 1,015—also consented to follow-up telephone interviews during which they answered a series of open-ended questions. Those responses were subsequently coded by staff at RDR.

For the phase two global study, the project team decided to forgo telephone follow-up interviews. Instead, key open-ended questions from phase one were incorporated into the online questionnaire. As a result, the questionnaire used in Europe, Asia, and Australia provided check box choices for what had been open-ended questions in the United States. Several factors led to the decision, most importantly the time required to translate and code open-ended responses.

Because of differences in the way these questions were presented in the two phases of the study, it is not appropriate to compare the U.S. responses on open-ended questions to the other responses.

## A Word on Sampling Error

No margin of error has been calculated for the results of the study because margin of error is meaningless except in the context of a random sample survey. For the Hudson Highland Center for High Performance study, random sampling would have required that every knowledge worker in a given population have an equal chance of being selected. Random sampling was not feasible for a study of this size and scope.

However, after examining the demographics of the knowledge workers who participated in the study, the research team concluded that the sample contains a broad range of people and that no one industry, occupation, age, or experience level dominates the results.

# Variations Among Knowledge Workers by Country and Region

In March 2003, nearly six hundred knowledge workers in the United States were interviewed for a study of workgroup performance that was conducted by the Hudson Highland Center for High Performance (CfHP) and the firm of Richard Day Research. The respondents were randomly selected from a group who earlier had completed an online survey and who gave permission to be contacted by telephone.

In October 2003, more than two thousand knowledge workers outside the United States took part in a global study that was conducted entirely online. One object of this global study was to determine whether knowledge workers share common experiences across countries, or if those in the United States are unique.

Analysis revealed a global standard of characteristics that distinguish high-performing workgroups. What follows are some specific findings, broken out by country.

## Australia

In Australia, 214 knowledge workers completed the online survey.

### Demographic Description of Australian Respondents

- **Occupation:** Medical professionals made up a greater proportion of knowledge workers in Australia (17 percent) than in the overall global sample (5.2 percent).
- **Sector and Industry:** Forty-three percent worked for publicly traded companies, 33 percent for privately held professional services firms, and 22 percent in the public sector. Looking at specific industries, the greatest numbers were in found in government (18 percent), professional/business systems (12 percent), finance (11 percent), and utilities (11 percent).
- **Workgroup Size:** The median size of an Australian workgroup was 24.5 employees, smaller than the global average of 30.
- **Managerial Responsibility:** Fifty-five percent of survey respondents reported that they manage someone, which is less than the global percentage (61 percent). Australian managers also tended to manage fewer employees than the global average.
- **Length of Tenure:** Australian respondents were newer to their organization and their workgroup than the global respondents as a whole. Specifically, 16 percent of Australian respondents were new to their organi-

zation, compared to 10 percent for global knowledge workers.

- **Age:** The average age of participating Australian knowledge workers was 40, close to the global figure (39.4).
- **Gender:** Seventy-five percent of respondents were men, just about the global average.
- **Income:** The majority of the Australian respondents made between the minimum eligible salary of $59,000 and $88,999 (Australian) annually.
- **Education:** Globally, the minimum criterion for inclusion in the study was a bachelor's degree or that country's equivalent. In Australia, 50 percent had the minimum—a university degree/bachelor's—while the other half had more education.

## Highlights of the Australian Findings

- A higher percentage of Australian knowledge workers consider themselves part of a high-performing workgroup than the global average (88 percent vs. 77 percent globally).
- Australia resembles the rest of the world when it comes to performance in specific areas. Sixty-four percent of the respondents gave evidence of excellent group performance in at least one of eight areas. This is almost exactly the global average of 62 percent.
- Using the CfHP definition of high performance (see Appendix 1), in Australia, only 7 percent of knowledge workers qualify as working in high-performing

workgroups. The global average is 10 percent. More than one-third of Australian knowledge workers are in nonperforming workgroups.

· Reported innovation in Australia is about the same as the rest of the world (49 percent compared to 53 percent globally). While the percentage reporting process innovation is similar to the global average, the percentage reporting product/service innovation is lower.

· On the 47-question Performance Scorecard (see Appendix 1), Australian knowledge workers have the largest gaps in the ratings between top performers and nonperformers.

· In Australia, only 42 percent of respondents agree that their company supports high performance, much less than the global average (58 percent). A majority (60 percent) agree that their group leader supports high performance, but the global average is even higher, at 70 percent.

## China (Beijing/Shanghai)

As noted in Appendix 1, China presented a number of challenges to the CfHP study. After much deliberation, the project team decided to limit the study to Beijing and Shanghai, where 291 knowledge workers completed the online survey. These large and important cities account for a relatively large proportion of the knowledge workers in China, although there is no way to know how closely they represent China as a whole. For that reason, references to China below should be understood as referring only to these two cities.

## Demographic Description of Beijing/Shanghai Respondents

- **Occupation:** Managers of large groups (more than 15 employees) and those involved in sales/marketing/advertising (26 percent and 23 percent respectively) were more highly represented in China than globally.

- **Sector and Industry:** Forty-nine percent worked in an enterprise that was at least partially government owned. Only 12 percent reported working for publicly traded companies with no government ownership.

- **Workgroup Size:** With 30 employees, Chinese workgroups fell at the median number for all workgroups in the global study.

- **Managerial Responsibility:** Seventy-one percent of survey respondents reported that they manage someone, which is higher than the global figure (61 percent); however, Chinese managers tended to manage a greater number of employees.

- **Length of Tenure:** Chinese respondents had less tenure with their organization than the global respondents as a whole. Fourteen percent were new to their organization, compared to 10 percent for global knowledge workers with 0–5 years in the organization.

- **Age:** Knowledge workers in China were much younger

than in the rest of the world, with 75 percent under 35 years old.

- **Gender:** Thirty-five percent of the Chinese respondents were women, higher than the global average of 23 percent.
- **Income:** The majority of the respondents (57 percent) made between 170,000 yuan (the screening minimum) and 199,000 yuan annually. The rest had higher incomes.
- **Education:** Globally, the minimum criterion for inclusion in the study was a bachelor's degree or that country's equivalent. Seventy-nine percent of Chinese respondents had the minimum (similar to the Australian university degree/bachelor's), while twenty-one percent had more education.

## Highlights of the Beijing/Shanghai Findings

- The great majority of China's knowledge workers consider themselves part of a high-performing workgroup (87 percent vs. 77 percent globally).
- A 79 percent majority of Beijing/Shanghai respondents gave evidence of excellent group performance in at least one of eight areas. This is significantly higher than the global average of 62 percent, and higher than any other nation in the study.
- Using the CfHP definition of high performance, 17 percent of Beijing/Shanghai knowledge workers

qualify as working in high-performing workgroups. This is the highest percentage of any country in the study.

- Innovation in China is higher than in any other country studied, in both product and system innovation.
- On the 47-question Performance Scorecard, Chinese knowledge workers consistently rate their workgroups higher on each characteristic than the overall global average. In fact, Beijing/Shanghai knowledge workers scored themselves higher than those in any other country examined.
- In Beijing/Shanghai, 76 percent agree that their organization supports high performance, much higher than the global average of 58 percent. Seventy-eight percent also agree that their group leader supports high performance.

## France

In France, 278 knowledge workers completed the online survey.

### Demographic Description of French Respondents

- **Occupation:** Twenty-four percent of respondents were managers, which is comparable to the global average; twenty-one percent were engineers or architects, somewhat higher than the global average.

- **Sector and Industry:** Forty-nine percent worked in publicly traded companies; 15 percent worked in government (comparable to the rest of Europe); 18 percent in finance; and 16 percent for computer or electronics firms.

- **Workgroup Size:** The median size of a French workgroup was 21 employees, lower than the global average of 30.

- **Managerial Responsibility:** Seventy percent of French respondents reported that they manage someone—higher than the global total of 61 percent—but French managers tended to manage fewer employees than those from other countries.

- **Length of Tenure:** French respondents were about the same as global respondents in their average tenure with both their organization (9 years) and their workgroup (4.6 years).

- **Age:** Knowledge workers in France skewed slightly younger than the rest of the world, with 60 percent between 31 and 45 years old.

- **Gender:** The French respondents included slightly more women than other countries (27 percent compared to 23 percent globally).

- **Income:** The majority of the French respondents (62 percent) made between €45,000 and €60,000 annually.

- **Education:** Globally, the minimum criterion for inclusion in the study was a bachelor's degree or that country's equivalent. In the French case, 79 percent of respondents had attained an educational level of at least BAC+4, the equivalent of a U.S. bachelor's degree.

## Highlights of the French Findings

- Most French knowledge workers consider themselves part of a high-performing workgroup (72 percent vs. 77 percent globally), but less so than in the rest of Europe.
- Sixty-two percent of French respondents gave evidence of excellent group performance in at least one of eight areas. This is identical to the overall global average.
- Using the CfHP definition of high performance, only 8 percent of French knowledge workers qualify as working in high-performing workgroups, somewhat lower than the 10 percent global average.
- Innovation in France was about the same as the global average (51 percent compared to 53 percent globally). French workers tended to be lower in reported product/service innovation.
- On the 47-question Performance Scorecard, French knowledge workers tended to rate their workgroups about the same as the global averages.
- In France, only 48 percent agree that their organization supports high performance, a figure that is much lower than the global average of 58 percent. While 61 percent agree that their group leader supports high performance, this too is lower than the global average (70 percent).

## Germany

In Germany, 265 knowledge workers completed the online survey.

### Demographic Description of German Respondents

- **Occupation:** Compared to global averages, an average number of respondents were managers (25 percent) and IT professionals/programmers (20 percent).
- **Sector and Industry:** A disproportionately high number of respondents (27 percent) worked in large, privately owned companies. Relatively few worked for government, compared to the rest of Europe. Twenty-two percent worked for computer or electronics firms, 14 percent in financial institutions, and 13 percent in information/advertising.
- **Workgroup Size:** German workgroups were among the smallest in the study, with a median size of 13 employees. More than half the respondents reported working in groups with fewer than 15 employees.
- **Managerial Responsibility:** Fifty-six percent of German survey respondents reported that they manage someone, five percentage points lower than the global total; however, German managers tended to manage slightly fewer employees than the overall average.
- **Length of Tenure:** German respondents had longer tenure with both their organization and their workgroup than the global respondents as a whole. Only 6

percent of German respondents were new to their organization, compared to 10 percent for global knowledge workers.

- **Age:** The average age of German knowledge workers was 39 years old, closely resembling the rest of the world.
- **Gender:** The German respondents were overwhelmingly male (86 percent compared to the 77 percent global average).
- **Income:** 35 percent of the German respondents made between €45,000 and €60,000 annually, and 40 percent made between €60,000 and €80,000. The rest made more than €80,000 per year.
- **Education:** Globally, the minimum criterion for inclusion in the study was a bachelor's degree or that country's equivalent. In Germany, 88 percent of respondents were university graduates and 12 percent had postgraduate education.

## Highlights of the German Findings

- Most German knowledge workers consider themselves part of a high-performing workgroup (86 percent vs. 77 percent globally).
- Seventy-one percent of German respondents gave evidence of excellent group performance in at least one of eight areas. This is somewhat higher than the global average of 62 percent.
- Using the CfHP definition of high performance, 12 percent of German knowledge workers qualify as

working in high-performing workgroups. This is slightly higher than the global average.

- Innovation in Germany was nearly identical to the global average (54 percent compared to 53 percent globally). The level of product/service innovation was among the highest of all countries studied.

- On the 47-question Performance Scorecard, German knowledge workers tended to rate their workgroups higher than the global averages.

- In Germany, only 48 percent agree that their organization supports high performance, much lower than the global average of 58 percent. While 61 percent agree that their group leader supports high performance, this figure too is lower than the global average.

## Italy

In Italy, 89 knowledge workers completed the online survey. It was very difficult to find knowledge workers in Italy, using the same methods, panel vendor, and screening criteria as the rest of Europe.

### Demographic Description of Italian Respondents
- **Occupation:** A higher percentage of knowledge workers in Italy were managers than elsewhere in Europe (33 percent compared to the European average of 27

percent). And medical professionals accounted for 26 percent of knowledge workers, a number far higher than in any other country examined.

- **Sector and Industry:** Thirty-four percent worked in government service, double the European average. Only 28 percent worked for publicly traded firms.

- **Workgroup Size:** The median size of an Italian workgroup was 29 employees, reflecting the global average.

- **Managerial Responsibility:** Eighty-three percent of Italian respondents reported that they manage someone, higher than the global average (61 percent); however, Italian managers tended to manage slightly fewer employees.

- **Length of Tenure:** Italian respondents had longer tenure with both their organization and their workgroup than the global respondents as a whole. Only 7 percent of Italian respondents were new to their organization and to their workgroup, compared to 10 percent and 22 percent respectively for global knowledge workers.

- **Age:** Knowledge workers in Italy skewed somewhat older than the rest of the world, with 72 percent between 36 and 55 years old. Compared to other countries, there were few Italian workers in the 18 to 30 age range.

- **Gender:** Eighty percent of Italian respondents were men.

- **Income:** The majority of the Italian respondents (53 percent) made between €45,000 and €60,000 annually, reflecting the European average for countries that have adopted the euro.
- **Education:** Globally, the minimum criterion for inclusion in the study was a bachelor's degree or that country's equivalent. In Italy, 78 percent had achieved a Laurea, and the remainder had even more education.

## Highlights of the Italian Findings

- Italian knowledge workers are slightly less likely to consider themselves part of a high-performing workgroup than the rest of the world (73 percent vs. 77 percent globally).
- Sixty-six percent of Italian respondents gave evidence of excellent group performance in at least one of eight areas. This is slightly higher than the overall global average (62 percent).
- Using the CfHP definition of high performance, 9 percent of Italian knowledge workers qualify as working in high-performing workgroups, slightly lower than the 10 percent global average.
- Italians reported a lower level of innovation than the global average (48 percent compared to 53 percent).
- On the 47-question Performance Scorecard, knowledge workers in Italy tended to rate their workgroups about the same as did all European respondents.
- In Italy, only 48 percent agree that their organization

supports high performance, much lower than the global average of 58 percent. However, 72 percent agree that their group leader supports high performance, slightly higher than the global average.

## Japan

In Japan, 294 knowledge workers completed the online survey.

### Demographic Description of Japanese Respondents

- **Occupation:** Engineers made up a greater proportion of knowledge workers in Japan (26 percent) than in the overall global sample (15.6 percent).
- **Sector and Industry:** Respondents came from a broad range of professional occupations and industries, and the majority reported working for publicly traded companies. Relatively few worked in the government sector. Twenty-three of the 52 largest Japanese corporations were represented, including Honda, NTT, Sony, Mitsubishi, Matsushita, Hitachi, Sharp, Bridgestone, Toshiba, Tokyo Gas, and Nippon Steel. Twenty-four percent of respondents worked in the industrial/manufacturing sector and 23 percent in computer/electronics. This represents a somewhat higher proportion of knowledge workers in manufacturing than elsewhere.

- **Workgroup Size:** Japanese workgroups were the largest that were reported. The median size of a Japanese workgroup was 50 employees, and more than half of the respondents said they worked in groups with more than 35 employees.

- **Managerial Responsibility:** Sixty-one percent of the respondents reported that they manage someone, which equals the global total; however, Japanese managers tended to manage fewer employees.

- **Length of Tenure:** Japanese respondents had longer tenure with both their organization and their workgroup than the global respondents as a whole (14.4 years in the organization, compared to 9 years globally). Only 5 percent of Japanese respondents were new to their organization, compared to 10 percent for global knowledge workers.

- **Age:** Knowledge workers in Japan skewed somewhat older than the rest of the world, with 53 percent between 36 and 45 years old. Globally 37 percent were in that age range.

- **Gender:** The Japanese respondents were almost exclusively men (95 percent), a figure that is much higher than the 77 percent global average.

- **Income:** The majority of the respondents made between ¥6 million and ¥8 million annually.

- **Education:** Globally, the minimum criterion for inclusion in the study was a bachelor's degree or that country's equivalent. Seventy-seven percent had

Japan's minimum criterion for inclusion, a university degree. The rest had more education.

## Highlights of the Japanese Findings

- Comparatively few Japanese knowledge workers consider themselves part of a high-performing workgroup (48 percent vs. 77 percent globally). It is also noteworthy that 27 percent of the Japanese respondents said they are in groups that used to be high performing but are no longer. The global average is 11 percent.

- Japan lags behind the rest of the world in performance in specific areas. Forty-five percent of respondents gave evidence of excellent group performance in at least one of eight areas. This is significantly lower than the global average of 62 percent, and lower than in any single nation studied.

- Using the CfHP definition of high performance, 5 percent of Japanese knowledge workers qualify as working in high-performing workgroups. Again, this is the lowest percentage of all countries studied. A majority of Japanese knowledge workers are in workgroups with no performance evidence at all.

- Innovation in Japan lags behind virtually every other country studied, especially when it comes to product/service innovation.

- On the 47-question Performance Scorecard, Japanese knowledge workers consistently rate their workgroups lower on each characteristic than the overall global averages. In fact, Japanese knowledge workers score themselves lower than those in any other country examined. While this may be cultural, it also reflects the very low level of high performance seen in Japan.

- Only 48 percent of Japanese respondents agree that their company supports high performance, somewhat less than the global average. A majority agree that their group leader supports high performance, but not as many as the global average.

## The Netherlands

In the Netherlands, 187 knowledge workers completed the online survey.

### Demographic Description of Dutch Respondents

- **Occupation:** Compared to global averages, a much higher percentage of Dutch knowledge workers were managers (41 percent compared to the European average of 27 percent). 18 percent of the respondents were programmers/IT professionals.
- **Sector and Industry:** Fifty-one percent worked in publicly traded companies, higher than the European average; 20 percent were involved with financial firms; and 14 percent with industrial or manufacturing firms.
- **Workgroup Size:** The median size of a Dutch workgroup was 28 employees, among the largest in Europe.

- **Managerial Responsibility:** 62 percent of respondents reported that they manage someone, which reflects the global total; however, Dutch workers manage a larger number of employees.
- **Length of Tenure:** Dutch respondents had longer tenure with their organization (13 years) than the global respondents as a whole (9 years). Only 6 percent of Dutch respondents were new to their organization, compared to 10 percent for global knowledge workers.
- **Age:** Knowledge workers in the Netherlands skewed somewhat older than the rest of the world, with 67 percent between 36 and 45 years old. The percentage of Dutch workers 56 and older was more than double the global percentage.
- **Gender:** The Dutch respondents were largely men (86 percent compared to 77 percent globally).
- **Income:** The majority of the Dutch respondents (50 percent) made between €45,000 and €60,000 annually.
- **Education:** Globally, the minimum criterion for inclusion in the study was a bachelor's degree or that country's equivalent. In the case of the Netherlands, respondents were divided among HBO/Middelbaaronderwijs (32 percent), post-HBO-onderwijs/Hogerunderwijs (32 percent), Universiteit (27 percent), and post-universiteit/post-universitair (10 percent).

## Highlights of the Dutch Findings

- Dutch knowledge workers are about as likely to consider their workgroup high performing as workers from the rest of the globe (78 percent vs. 77 percent).
- Fifty-eight percent of Dutch respondents gave evidence of excellent group performance in at least one of eight areas. This is slightly lower than the overall global average of 62 percent.
- Using the CfHP definition of high performance, 9 percent of Dutch knowledge workers qualify as working in high-performing workgroups, slightly lower than the 10 percent global average.
- Innovation in the Netherlands is higher than the global average (60 percent, compared to 53 percent). Dutch respondents lagged in reporting profit/revenue growth. They scored higher on process innovation than in product/service innovation.
- On the 47-question Performance Scorecard, knowledge workers in the Netherlands tended to rate their workgroups higher than the overall European average.
- In the Netherlands, only 49 percent agree that their organization supports high performance, much lower than the global average of 58 percent. While 63 percent agree that their group leader supports high performance, this too is lower than the global average.

## Sweden

In Sweden, 164 knowledge workers completed the online survey.

### Demographic Description of Swedish Respondents

- **Occupation:** A higher percentage of Swedish knowledge workers were managers than the European average (33 percent, compared to 27 percent). Nineteen percent of the respondents were programmers/IT professionals.
- **Sector and Industry:** Forty-nine percent worked in publicly traded companies, higher than the global average (44 percent). Swedish respondents came from a range of industries: Twelve percent were involved in the health field (higher than the global average), 13 percent worked for industrial or manufacturing firms (higher than the global average), 16 percent in the computer/electronics sector, and 14 percent in financial services.
- **Workgroup Size:** Swedish respondents reported comparatively small workgroups. The median size of a Swedish workgroup was 12 employees; more than half of the respondents said they worked in groups with 15 or fewer employees.
- **Managerial Responsibility:** Seventy-eight percent of survey respondents reported that they manage someone, which exceeds the global total. However, Swedish

managers tended to manage fewer employees than the global average.

- **Length of Tenure:** Swedish respondents had longer tenure with their organization and their workgroup than the global respondents as a whole. Only 8 percent of Swedish respondents were new to their organization, compared to 10 percent for global knowledge workers.
- **Age:** Knowledge workers in Sweden skewed somewhat older than the rest of the world, with 58 percent between 36 and 55 years old.
- **Gender:** The Swedish respondents were largely men (86 percent compared to the 77 percent global average).
- **Income:** The majority of the Swedish respondents (62 percent) made between €45,000 and €60,000 annually.
- **Education:** Globally, the minimum criterion for inclusion in the study was a bachelor's degree or that country's equivalent. Fifty-seven percent of the respondents had Sweden's minimum criterion for inclusion, the *Mellangang eftergymnasial utbildning.* The rest had more education.

## Highlights of the Swedish Findings

- Swedish knowledge workers are less likely than global knowledge workers to consider themselves part of a high-performing workgroup (73 percent vs. 77 percent).
- Fifty-four percent of Swedish respondents gave evi-

dence of excellent group performance in at least one of eight areas. This is lower than the overall global average (62 percent).

- Using the CfHP definition of high performance, only 6 percent of Swedish knowledge workers qualify as working in high-performing workgroups. Of all the countries/regions examined, only Japan was lower.

- Innovation in Sweden is quite low (38 percent compared to 53 percent reporting innovation globally). Sweden ranks last in reporting process innovation and near the bottom in reporting product/service innovation.

- On the 47-question Performance Scorecard, knowledge workers in Sweden tended to rate their workgroups higher than all European respondents, despite the low level of high-performing organizations actually found.

- In Sweden, 61 percent agree that their organization supports high performance, slightly higher than the global average of 58 percent. Even more (77 percent) agree that their group leader supports high performance.

## United Kingdom

In the United Kingdom (England, Wales, Scotland, and Northern Ireland), 307 knowledge workers completed the online survey.

## *Demographic Description of United Kingdom Respondents*

- **Occupation:** Compared to global figures, an average number of managers participated (26 percent) and a disproportionate number of financial analysts participated (16 percent compared to 8 percent globally).

- **Sector and Industry:** Fifty percent worked in an enterprise that was publicly traded, higher than the European average of 44 percent. The greatest number of U.K. knowledge workers were found in the finance (23 percent) and computer/electronics (14 percent) segments. This represents a somewhat higher representation in finance than elsewhere in the study.

- **Workgroup Size:** U.K. respondents operated in large workgroups—the median size was 40 employees, and more than half of the respondents reported that they worked in groups with more than 35 employees.

- **Managerial Responsibility:** Seventy-three percent of the respondents reported that they manage someone, which surpasses the global total. However, U.K. managers tended to manage fewer employees.

- **Length of Tenure:** U.K. respondents had less tenure with both their organization and their workgroup than the global respondents as a whole. Sixteen percent were new to their organization (one year or less), compared to 10 percent for global knowledge workers.

- **Age:** The average age of knowledge workers in the U.K. was 40 years old, reflecting the global average.

- **Gender:** Seventy-six percent of the U.K. respondents were men, nearly the same as the global average.
- **Income:** The majority of the respondents made between £40,000 and £55,000 annually, and a high percentage (25 percent) earned more than £70,000 per year.
- **Education:** Globally, the minimum criterion for inclusion in the study was a bachelor's degree or that country's equivalent. In the U.K., 80 percent reported graduate or postgraduate education.

## Highlights of the United Kingdom Findings

- U.K. knowledge workers tended to consider themselves part of a high-performing workgroup (85 percent vs. 77 percent globally).
- 69 percent of U.K. respondents gave evidence of excellent group performance in at least one of eight areas. This is somewhat higher than the global average of 62 percent.
- Using the CfHP definition of high performance, 10 percent of U.K. knowledge workers qualify as working in high-performing workgroups. This is the same as the global average.
- Innovation in the U.K. lags somewhat behind the global average (48 percent compared to 53 percent). This is the case with both product and system innovation.
- On the 47-question Performance Scorecard, U.K.

knowledge workers tended to rate their workgroups slightly higher on average compared to the global numbers.

· In the U.K., only 42 percent agree that their organization supports high performance, much lower than the global average of 58 percent. While 60 percent agree that their group leader supports high performance, this is also lower than the global average.

## United States

In the United States, 1,015 knowledge workers completed the online survey. Subsequently, 592 of them were interviewed by telephone.

### Demographic Description of United States Respondents

· **Occupation:** Compared to other nations, an average number of managers (24 percent) participated. Twenty-two percent of the U.S. respondents were IT professionals/programmers, 15 percent were in engineering/architecture, and 12 percent each were in sales/marketing and finance.

· **Sector and Industry:** The U.S. study excluded government employees, so all respondents worked either for a publicly traded company (84 percent) or a large professional services firm (16 percent). Industries with the highest representation were computer/electronics (23 percent), finance (18 percent), industrial/manufacturing (12 percent), and health care/pharmaceutical (12 percent). Employees from more than half of the Fortune 100 were represented.

- **Workgroup Size:** The median workgroup size in the United States was 25. Almost one-quarter of respondents worked in groups with more than 125 people.

- **Managerial Responsibility:** Half of the knowledge workers managed others, which was lower than other nations examined. The average number of people they reported managing was 15.

- **Length of Tenure:** On average, respondents had been with their company almost 8 years and with their current workgroup for 4.3 years. Twelve percent were new to their company (one year or less), and 22 percent were new to their workgroup.

- **Age:** The average age of U.S. knowledge workers was 39 years old. Seventeen percent were under 30 years old.

- **Gender:** Thirty-seven percent of the U.S. knowledge workers were women, higher than the global average.

- **Income:** The average income of knowledge workers was $92,000. Thirty percent earned more than $100,000 annually.

- **Education:** Globally, the minimum criterion for inclusion in the study was a bachelor's degree or that country's equivalent. Sixty-three percent in the U.S.

survey had the minimum of a bachelor's degree, and 37 percent had even more education.

## Highlights of the United States Findings

- Most U.S. knowledge workers consider themselves part of a high-performing workgroup (89 percent vs. 77 percent globally).
- Sixty-one percent of U.S. respondents gave evidence of excellent group performance in at least one of eight areas. This is just about the global average of 62 percent.
- Using the CfHP definition of high performance, 11 percent of U.S. knowledge workers qualify as working in high-performing workgroups. This is slightly above the global average of 10 percent.
- Reported innovation in the United States was right at the global average (53 percent).
- On the 47-question Performance Scorecard, U.S. knowledge workers tended to rate their organizations similarly on most measures compared to the ratings given by global knowledge workers.
- In the United States, 78 percent agreed that their organization supports high performance, much higher than the global average of 58 percent. An even higher percentage (87 percent) agree that their group leader supports high performance.

Knowledge workers from the following companies participated in the U.S. study:

Abbott Laboratories

Accenture

Acclaim Entertainment

ACS (Affiliated Computer Services)

Acxiom Inc.

ADESA Impact

ADP (Automatic Data Processing, Inc.)

Aetna Life

AG Edwards & Sons, Inc.

Agilent Technologies

Alcatel USA, Inc.

Alliant Energy

Allstate Insurance

ALZA Corporation

Amcast Industrial Corporation

American Airlines

American Express

American Management Systems, Inc.

AmeriPath Inc.

Amersham Biosciences

AOL Time Warner

Aon Corporation

Applied Materials, Inc.

Apropos Technology

Araphel Consulting, LLC

Aspen Systems

AstraZeneca

Astro-Med, Inc.

AT&T

Autodesk

Avaya Inc.

Aventis

Avnet Inc.

AXA Advisors

Bacou-Dalloz

Bank of America

Banta Corporation

Barnes & Noble

Baxter Healthcare

BEA Systems

Bear Stearns

Bell Atlantic

BellSouth

Benchmark Electronics, Inc.

Benefit Services, Inc.

Best Software, Inc.

BOC Temescal

Boeing

Boise Office Solutions

The Boston Company

Boston Scientific

Brinks

BAE Systems (British Aerospace Engineering Systems)

Broadcom Corporation

Brown & James

Buck Consultants

Cadence Design Systems

Callaway Golf

Caronia Corp.

Caterpillar Inc.

Cendant

Ceridian

Cessna Aircraft

Charles Schwab & Company

Chevron Texaco

Chubb Insurance

CIBER, Inc.

CIENA Corporation

CIGNA Corp.

The CIT Group

Citibank

CitiFinancial

Citigroup

The Clipper Group

Clorox Company

CMS Energy Corp.

CNA

Cobalt Corporation

Coldwell Banker

Compass Banker

CompUSA

Computer Aid, Inc.

Computer Associates International, Inc.

Compuware

Cookson Group PLC

Cooper Tire

Coughlin Logistics

Council 12 Computing

Counter Technology Incorporated

Co Vest Banc

Creative Automation

Credit Lyonnais America

Credit Suisse First Boston

CSC (Computer Sciences Corporation)

CSX

CTG

CTS Interconnect Systems

Cummins Inc.

Dana Corporation

Daugherty Systems

Deloitte & Touche

DENTSPLY Austenal
Diebold Inc.
DIRECTV
Disney
Diversified Investment
    Advisors
Dominion Virginia Power
Duff & Phelps, LLC
Dun & Bradstreet
DuPont
Eckerd
Ecosphere Technologies
EDS (Electronic Data
    Systems)
Edwards Lifesciences
Elk Corp.
EMC Corporation
EnerCom Inc.
ENGlobal
Ericsson
Experio Solutions
Express
Exult
FactSet Research Systems
Fairfield Resorts, Inc.
Farmers Insurance Group
Fastenal
FCG Consulting

Federal Express
Federal-Mogul
Federated Department
    Stores, Inc.
Fidelity Investments
Fireman's Funds
    Insurance Company
First Centennial Bank
First Health
First International Bank
    and Trust
Fletcher Allen Health Care
Franklin Electric
Franklin Resources, Inc.,
    and its subsidiary
    Fiduciary Trust
Fresenius Medical Care
    North America (Spectra
    Laboratories)
Gannett Company, Inc.
Gartner
GE Healthcare Financial
    Services
Genencor International
Genentech, Inc.
General Dynamics
General Electric
General Mills

General Physics Corp.

Genesis Health Centers

Genuine Parts Corp.

Gevity HR

GfK Custom Research, Inc.

GIII Leather Fashions

GlaxoSmithKline

Goldman Sachs

Great-West Life

Greenfield

Greenville Memorial
  Hospital

GTECH Corporation

GTSI (Government
  Technology Services)

Hallmark Cards

Harmonic, Inc.

Harris Bank

Harris Interactive

Harsco Corporation

Hartford Technology Ser-
  vices Company

Healthcare Corporation of
  America

HealthSouth Total Body
  Scan

Hewitt Associates

Hewlett-Packard

Hill's Pet Nutrition

Hilti Inc. of the Hilti Group

Hilton Hotels Corp.

Hipotronics, Inc.

Hirose Electric USA

Hitachi Innovative
  Solutions

H.J. Heinz

Home Depot

Honeywell

Hoover, a division of
  Maytag

Horizon Mental Health
  Management

Household International

HSA Commercial

Hughes Associates

Hummingbird USA, Inc.

Hyperion Solutions, Corp.

IBM

IET (Industrial
  Engineering
  Technologies)

IMS Health

Industrial Bank of Japan

ING

Innovex, Inc.

Inovant

The Institute for Genomic
Research
Integral Systems, Inc.
Integraph Corporation
Intel Corporation
International
Environmental Corp.
Intervoice
Invitrogen Corporation
ITS
JPMorgan Chase and
Company
Jack in the Box, Inc.
J. D. Edwards
Johnson & Johnson
Johnson Controls, Inc.
Kaye Scholer
KDN Data Corporation
Kemper Insurance
Kent Automotive
KGA-CMS
King & Spalding
Knowledge Networks
Kodak
KPMG
LBCA
Lenox
LexisNexis

Liberty Insurance Services
Liberty Regional Agency
Markets
Lincoln Property Company
Lions Gate Entertainment
Liquent Inc.
Lithia Foothills Dodge
Chrysler Jeep
Lockheed Martin
Lorillard Tobacco Company
Lowe's Companies
LSI Logic Corporation
Lucent Technologies
MACTEC
McKesson Corporation
McKinsey & Company
Madison Gas & Electric
Company
Maimonides Medical
Center
Manchester Technologies,
Inc.
Manpower Inc.
ManTech International
Corporation
Manugistics
MapInfo
Marsh USA, Inc.

MCI

Mellon Financial
 Corporation

Merck & Co., Inc.

Meridian Financial Services

Merrill Lynch

Metco Health

Metropolitan Life
 Insurance Co.

MFS

Micro Motions

Micron Technology, Inc.

MICROS Systems, Inc.

Microsoft Corporation

Mindshare (traded under
 WPP Group)

Module USA

Morrison's Management
 Specialists

Motive Communications

Motorola, Inc.

Nalley Motor Trucks

Nationwide Provident

Navigator Systems Inc.

NCR

Nelnet

New Horizon

New Horizons Worldwide

New World Restaurant
 Group Inc.

NFO

Northern Trust

Northrim Bank

Northrop Grumman

Novartis Pharmaceutical

Nuclear Management Inc.

NUI

Nuveen Investments

NVC

Ocean Spray

Ogilvy Public Relations

Optum, Inc.

Oracle Corporation

Osmonics Corp.

PAREXEL International

PBGC (Pension Benefit-
 Guaranty Corporation)

Pearson Education

Pediatric Services of
 America

PETsMART

Pfizer

Physicians Advantage Ser-
 vices

Pioneer Electronics

Pitney Bowes

Playmates Toys, Inc.
PPD
Pratt & Whitney
PricewaterhouseCoopers
Princess Cruises
Principal Financial Group
Procter and Gamble
Professional Publishing
    Group, a division of
    Reed Elsevier
Prudential
PSEG Nuclear
Putnam Investments
Qiagen, Inc.
Quebecor World
Qwest
Raymond James
Retalix
Reuters
Rhodia
RiteAid Corporation
Roche Laboratories
Rockwell Collins
Rohm and Haas
Rural/Metro Corporation
SAIC (Science Applications
    International
    Corporation)

Sanford Rose Opportunity
    Center
Sanofi-Synthelabo, Inc.
SBC
SCA Tissue
Schering-Plough Corp.
SchlumbergerSema
Schmeltzer, Aptaker, &
    Shepard
Scott Hospitality Services
Seagate Technology
Seitel, Inc.
Sempra Energy
Shell Oil Products
Shook, Hardy & Bacon
The Shutter Mill, Inc.
Siemens Nixdorf
Silicon Image
Silicon Systems
    Electronics Corporation
Silliker
Simon Property Group
SoftAd
SMCI (Software
    Management Consul-
    tants, Inc.)
Solectron
Sony Electronics

Sony-Ericsson
Southern Graphic Systems
Sprint
Staffmark
State Bank of Long Island
State Farm
State Street, Inc.
Stewart Title
STMicroelectronics
Storage Technology
Strategy XXI Group, Ltd.
Sun Microsystems
SunTrust Bank, Inc.
Sybas Incorporated
Systems and Computer
    Technology, Inc.
T. Rowe Price
Targetbase
TBWA/Chiat/Day
Telcordia Technologies
Telelogic
Teradyne Inc.
Texas Instruments
Thomson Financial
Thousand Trails, Inc.
3D/International
3M
Tier Technologies

TIG Insurance
Time Inc.
TK Shipping, Ltd.
TMA Corporation
TNS (Taylor Nelson Sofres)
Tolland Bank
TOWER Automotive
Triad Hospitals, Inc.
    (Northwest Health
    System)
Tribune Company
Trimble Navigation
Triumph Composite
    Systems, Inc.
Tumbleweed
    Communications
Turner Entertainment
UBS
UMB Bank
Unisys Corporation
UnitedHealth Group
UPS
U.S. Bancorp
UST
Valeo
Vanguard Group
Verizon Communications
Viking Components

Wachovia Corporation
Walgreens
Warner Brothers
WebMD
Wellpoint Pharmacy
    Management
Wells Fargo
Wells National Services
    Corporation
WestLB Systems
Williams-Sonoma, Inc.
Willis
WORC-TV Nexstar
    Communications
Worthington Industries
Wyeth
Xilinx
Zurich North America

# Factor Analysis

As part of the Hudson Highland Center for High Performance study of global knowledge workers (see Appendix 1), Richard Day Research conducted a factor analysis on responses to the forty-seven attributes that make up the study's Performance Scorecard.

Factor analysis is a statistical technique used to reduce the number of variables in a collection and classify them by determining the relationships among the variables. It identifies patterns of correlation and organizes those variables that correlate highly into clusters, called factors.

A factor is derived from a set of variables, drawn from the total collection, that respondents rate in a similar way. Analysts can infer the meaning of a factor from the degree of correlation between individual variables and the factor in question (factor "loading"). The higher a specific attribute correlates with a given factor, the more useful that variable can be in determining the meaning of the factor.

For example, a survey might ask a sample of voters their views about a large number of issues. Several individual items—say, support for increased defense spending, lower taxes, and prayer in public schools—might all have similar high correlations with one factor. A pollster interpreting the results might label that factor *conservatism*.

Factor analysis, then, can help extract the overarching themes that emerge from a collection of data. In many cases, the technique validates researchers' preconceptions, but it often forces researchers to rethink some of their assumptions.

For the study, the factor analysis was limited to those respondents identified as belonging to high-performing workgroups. The project team employed the statistical software application SPSS 11.5 for Windows to analyze the data. The analysis rendered eight factors from the set of forty-seven attributes.

By identifying features some of the themes had in common, the project team ultimately conflated them into the three principal high performance drivers discussed throughout this book: value people, optimize critical thinking, and seize opportunities.

# The Global Average

Results from the United States are not included in the global average reported in the text. U.S. respondents were asked open-ended questions about what their company does to stifle high performance. Of the total responses, Richard Day Research recorded the top three. Respondents outside the United States, (in Europe, Japan, Beijing/Shanghai, and Australia) were given an online survey and asked to check the statements that applied, with no limit. Because the method used to collect this data was different for the U.S. study, results were not combined. However, since there was little variance in the responses around the globe, we believe that the U.S. numbers would be comparable.

Butteriss, M. *Re-Inventing HR: Changing Roles to Create the High-Performance Organization.* San Francisco: Jossey-Bass, 1998.

Carnevale, D. B. *Trustworthy Government: Leadership and Management Strategies for Building Trust and High Performance.* San Francisco: Jossey-Bass, 1995.

Collins, Jim. *Good to Great: Why Some Companies Make the Leap . . . and Others Don't.* New York: Harper Business, 2001.

Conner, Daryl R. *Managing at the Speed of Change: How Resilient Managers Succeed and Prosper Where Others Fail.* New York: Random House, 1992.

Fisher, K. K. "Managing in the High-Commitment Workplace." *Organizational Dynamics,* 17:3 (1989), pp. 31–50.

Fletcher, J. *Patterns of High Performance: Discovering the Ways People Work Best.* San Francisco: Berrett-Koehler Publishers, 1993.

Goleman, Daniel, Richard Boyatzis, and Annie McKee. *Primal Leadership: Realizing the Power of Emotional Intelligence.* Boston: Harvard Business School Press, 2002.

Hanna, D. P. *Designing Organizations for High Performance.* Reading, Massachusetts: Addison-Wesley, 1988.

Harris, P. R. *High Performance Leadership: Strategies for Maximum Career Productivity.* Glenview, Illinois: Scott, Foresman and Company, 1993.

Hesselbein, Frances, and Rob Johnston. *On High Performance Organizations: A Leader to Leader Guide.* San Francisco: Jossey-Bass, 2002.

Hesselbein, Frances, Marshall Goldsmith, and Ian Somerville, eds. *Leading Beyond the Walls: How High-Performing Organizations Collaborate for Shared Success.* San Francisco: Jossey-Bass, 2001.

Hesselbein, Frances, and Paul M. Cohen, eds. *Leader to Leader: Enduring Insights on Leadership from the Drucker Foundation's Award Winning Journal.* San Francisco: Jossey-Bass, 1999.

Huselid, Mark A. "The Impact of Human Resource Management Practices on Turnover, Productivity, and Corporate Financial Performance." *Academy of Management Journal,* 38:3 (June 1995), pp. 635–72.

Juechter, W. M., C. Fischer, and R. J. Alford. "Five Conditions for High Performance Cultures." *Training and Development,* 52:5 (1998), pp. 63–7.

Katzenbach, Jon R. *Peak Performance: Aligning the Hearts and Minds of Your Employees.* Boston: Harvard Business School Press, 2000.

Kerzner, H. *In Search of Excellence in Project Management: Successful Practices in High Performance Organizations.* New York: Van Nostrand Reinhold, 1998.

Kirkman, Bradley L., Kevin B. Lowe, and Dianne P. Young. *High-Performance Work Organizations: Definitions, Practices, and an Annotated Bibliography.* Greensboro, North Carolina: Center for Creative Leadership, 1999.

Kouzes, James M., and Barry Z. Posner. *The Leadership Challenge: How to Keep Getting Extraordinary Things Done in Organizations.* San Francisco: Jossey-Bass, 1995.

Letts, Christine W., William P. Ryan, and Allen Grossman. *High Perfor-*

*mance Nonprofit Organizations: Managing Upstream for Greater Impact.* New York: John Wiley & Sons, 1998.

Mohrman, Susan Albers, Gerald E. Ledford, and Edward E. Lawler III. *Strategies for High Performance Organizations—The CEO Report: Employee Involvement, TQM, and Reengineering Programs in Fortune 1000 Corporations.* San Francisco: Jossey-Bass, 2001.

Neusch, D. R. and A. F. Siebenaler. *The High Performance Enterprise: Reinventing the People Side of Your Business.* San Francisco: Jossey-Bass, 1998.

Obloj, Krzysztof, Donald P. Cushman, and Andrzej K. Kozminski. *Winning: Continuous Improvement Theory in High-Performance Organizations.* New York: State University of New York Press, 1995.

Odden, A. and C. Busch. *Financing Schools for High Performance: Strategies for Improving the Use of Educational Resources.* San Francisco: Jossey-Bass, 1998.

Pasmore, W. A. *Creating Strategic Change: Designing the Flexible, High-Performing Organization.* New York: John Wiley & Sons, 1994.

Price Waterhouse Change Integration Team. *Better Change: Best Practices for Transforming Your Organization.* New York: McGraw-Hill, 1994.

Price Waterhouse Change Integration Team. *The Paradox Principles: How High-Performance Companies Manage Chaos, Complexity, and Contradiction to Achieve Superior Results.* Chicago: Irwin Professional, 1996.

Reich, Robert. "Leadership and the High Performance Organization." *Journal for Quality and Participation,* 17:2 (March 1994), pp. 6–11.

Schuster, Frederick E., et al. "Management Practice, Organization Climate, and Performance: An Exploratory Study." *Journal of Applied Behavioral Science,* 33:2 (June 1997), pp. 209–26.

Smith, K. *Make Success Measurable!: A Mindbook-Workbook for Setting Goals and Taking Action.* San Francisco: Jossey-Bass, 1999.

Stoltz, Paul G. *Adversity Quotient: Turning Obstacles into Opportunities.* New York: John Wiley & Sons, 1999.

Stoltz, Paul G. *Adversity Quotient @ Work: Make Everyday Challenges the Key to Your Success.* New York: HarperCollins, 2000.

Tierney, W. G. *Building the Responsive Campus: Creating High Performance Colleges and Universities.* Thousand Oaks, California: SAGE Publications, 1999.

Yeatts, D. E., and C. Hyten. *High-Performance Self-Managed Teams: A Comparison of Theory to Practice.* Thousand Oaks, California: SAGE Publications, 1998.

HD 58.9 .A545 2004
Annunzio, Susan.
Contagious success